RECORD OF THINGS HEARD FROM THE TREASURY OF THE EYE OF THE TRUE TEACHINGS

Record of things heard

From the Treasury of the Eye
of the True Teaching

*The Shōbōgenzō-zuimonki,
talks of Zen master Dogen,
as recorded by Zen master Ejo*

Translated by Thomas Cleary

PRAJÑĀ PRESS
BOULDER   1980

Prajñā Press
Great Eastern Book Company
P.O. Box 271
Boulder, Colorado 80306

ISBN 0-87773-743-6
Printed in the United States of America

LIBRARY OF CONGRESS CATALOGING IN PUBLICATION DATA

Dogen, 1200-1253.
  Record of things heard from the treasury of the eye of the
true teaching = a translation of the Shobogenzo-zuimonki.

  1. Sotoshu-Doctrines. I. Cleary, Thomas.
II. Title.
BQ9449.D654S5513 1978   294.3'927   78-13112
ISBN 0-87773-743-6 pbk.

CONTENTS

INTRODUCTION

The *Shobogenzo-zuimonki* is a collection of talks by the great Japanese Zen master Dogen (1200–1253) given during the first years of his teaching career. These talks were recorded by Ejo, one of Dogen's first disciples and later his foremost successor; subsequently, this collection became a popular Zen classic, a source of daily inspiration to generations of Zen practitioners.

Dogen was born to a noble family and received the finest education available in Japan at that time; as evidence of his extraordinary intellectual capacity, he is said to have started composing poetry in Chinese at the age of four, and he read the Chinese translation of Vasubandhu's Buddhist classic *Abhidharmakosha* at the age of nine. In his early teens Dogen renounced the life of a court noble and official, for which he had been groomed, and devoted himself to Buddhist studies. Ordained as a monk at fourteen, within a few years Dogen had read the entire Buddhist canon and finally forsook the corrupt Tendai school to study the new Zen teachings brought to Japan by the pilgrim Eisai.

Eisai had also been a Tendai Buddhist monk, and had gone to China to study, with the hope of reviving the decadent Tendai church in Japan; finding Ch'an (Zen) Buddhism the predominant form in China then, Eisai journeyed to China a second time and spent five years mastering the Zen teaching. If Dogen actually met Eisai, it must have been shortly before the old teacher died; after Eisai's death, Dogen spent some nine years studying Zen with Eisai's successor Myozen. Later, Dogen had nothing but praise for Eisai, and regarded Myozen as his sole worthy successor, but determined to go to China himself to study further.

Dogen had many interesting and enlightening experiences during his five year sojourn in China, some of which he recounts in the

Zuimonki. The most significant event of this period, however, was his meeting with Ju-ching, who was to become his teacher. Here Dogen finally realized enlightenment that completely emancipated his mind and body, and was recognized as a true successor to the Zen heritage. After two more years of advanced study with Ju-ching, Dogen returned to Japan in 1227.

Dogen first stayed for a time at Kennin monastery, where he had earlier studied Zen with Eisai and Myozen; subsequently, he spent several years at over a dozen different places offered to him by well-wishing donors. In 1233 he came to stay in the Kannondori-in, a cloister on the grounds of an old dilapidated temple in Uji, a suburb of Kyoto. It was here that Dogen began to teach and attract followers. In 1236 a meditation hall was built, and the renovated temple was named Kosho Horin. It is said that a congregation of some fifty monks gathered there, and Dogen taught there for ten years; this was the site of the talks recorded in the *Shobogenzo-zuimonki.*

In 1243, with increased harassment from local Tendai factions, Dogen sought out a new abode deep in the mountains of old Echizen, in what is known as "Snow Country." Here he founded Eihei monastery, which later became headquarters of the Soto school of Zen, as Dogen's succession came to be known. After about ten years at Eihei, Dogen returned to Kyoto a final time, seeking medical treatment for the illness which was shortly to claim his life.

Dogen left an enormous body of works, commensurate with his role as a teacher, reformer, and founder of a school for the practical application of the original principles of Buddhism as he has experienced them in the living tradition of Zen. He lamented the corruption of Buddhism in Japan, especially the perversion of religious learning into a vehicle for worldly gain; he considered the entire history of Buddhism in Japan to have been warped in this way, and endeavored to establish a new kind of training ground and a fresh approach to study, based only on the will for enlightenment. While Dogen is especially famous for his towering intellect, in the *Shobogenzo-zuimonki* we see the extraordinary depth of Dogen's will and the strength of his character.

Perhaps the most insistent themes of the *Zuimonki* are the "mind of the Way," poverty, and selflessness. The mind of the Way is the spirit of enlightenment, acting for the sake of the enlightenment of all beings, studying the Way for the sake of the Way itself, without any hidden selfish motives. The poverty which Dogen teaches is both physical and spiritual, meaning freedom from the entanglements of possessions and learned understanding. It is perhaps easier to understand why Dogen was so adamant on these points when we consider how the vast wealth of the Tendai church underlay so much political and religious competition. All the new Buddhist movements of Dogen's time—the Pure Land, Nichiren, and Rinzai Zen schools—were developed by monks who had broken away from the formalities of Tendai teachings and institutions, after long and exhaustive studies without enlightenment. Dogen adjured his students to give up the intellectual studies they had become habituated to, and to practice Buddhism with their whole bodies, to surrender spiritual pride and transcend even understanding.

While certain parts of the *Shobogenzo-zuimonki*, thus, are primarily applicable to monks, having been addressed to a certain audience under certain conditions, nevertheless, the underlying spirit of these talks is naturally universal, and their fundamental messages transcend the bounds of time and culture; bearing on essential issues of human being and effort, Zen Master Dogen's keen observations, his complete sincerity and unbending determination, can be a mirror and a guide for "a thousand generations."

NOTE TO THE TRANSLATION

The talks which form the *Shobogenzo-zuimonki* are not arranged in a rigid system, and contain evidence of later editing and rephrasing. The two texts used for this translation are the *rufubon*, or popular version, edited by Menzan Zuiho (1683–1769), a leading Soto Zen monk of his time; and the so-called Choenji book, based on a recension of 1380. This latter text has been published with an annotated modern Japanese translation by Mizuno Mieko (Tokyo, Chikuma Shobo, 1963). The meaningful contents of these two versions are substantially the same, although there are a number of differences of detail. The first book of the older version corresponds to the sixth book of the popular edition. The language of the older version has been modified in Menzan's edition, using current vocabulary and adding inflections to make the text more readable. The difference between the two texts is obvious to anyone reading them in the original, but for the most part is not critical to an English translation. The sectioning of this translation generally follows the Iwanami edition of the *rufubon* by Watsuji Tetsuro, while the internal paragraphing generally follows that of Mizuno's edition of the Choenji book. Significant variations and adjustments based on comparison of the two texts have been noted where differences are more than a matter of style or language.

BOOK I

1

ONE DAY HE SAID,

In the *Continued Biographies of Eminent Monks*[1] it is recorded that in the community of a certain meditation teacher there was a monk who used a golden image of Buddha as well as a relic[2] of Buddha in worship; even in the communal dormitory he always burned incense and prostrated himself [before them], honoring and making offerings to them.

Once the meditation teacher said to him, "The image and relic of Buddha which you revere will eventually be wrong for you."

The monk did not agree. The teacher said, "This is the doing of evil spirits; you should quickly throw them away."

As the monk departed in a rage, the teacher immediately shouted after him, "Open up the box and look!" Though angry, the monk opened up the box; when he looked inside, he saw a poisonous serpent lying there coiled up.

As I reflect upon this, although the images and relics of Buddha are the form and bones left behind by the Tathagata[3] and should therefore be respected, nevertheless, if you think you can become enlightened just by worshipping them, this is a false view. It is a cause of becoming possessed by the poisonous snake of temptation.[4]

Because the merit of the Buddha's Teachings is something already established, they should be a blessing to men and gods just the same as a living Buddha. In general, it is true that if you honor and make offerings to the realms of the Three Jewels,[5] faults will disappear and you will obtain merit; the action of evil dispositions will dissipate and you will realize the fruit of humanity or godhead as a result. But to think that you will thereby obtain realization of the truth, this is a biased view. Because one who is called a "Buddhist" follows the Buddha's Teaching in order to arrive directly at the station of Buddhahood, you should simply meditate and discern the Way in accordance with the Teaching. The true activity which accords with the Teaching is that which the monastery now has as its basis: sole occupation with sitting.[6] You should reflect on this.

2

He also said,

Just because disciplined behavior and vegetarian diet is to be maintained, yet if you therefore insist upon these as fundamental, establishing them as practice, and think that you can thereby attain the Way, this is also wrong. It is just that this is the conduct of the patchrobed monks,[1] the tradition of the sons of Buddha; and therefore we follow and practice it. Do not take this to be fundamental just because it is a good thing.

Yet I do not mean to say that you should therefore violate precepts and be self-indulgent. To cling in such a manner is an erroneous view; it is that of an outsider. We just conform because it is the standard of the Buddhist family and the tradition of the meditation halls. As for making it into the fundamental concern, however, when I was staying in the temples of China, I never saw such a thing. For the purpose of true attainment of the Way, effort in seated meditation alone is the tradition of the Buddhas and Patriarchs. For this reason a fellow student of mine, Gogenbo, who was a disciple of the Zen Master Eisai,[2] taught me to abandon rigid adherence to vegetarianism and continual recitation of the preceptual scripture[3] while in the meditation hall in China.

Ejo asked, "Should the standards for study of the Way in the monastery adhere to the Pure Rules of Pai Chang?[4] If so, I see that he considered the accepting and maintenance of precepts as prerequisite. Also, I see that the transmitted tradition hands down the 'Fundamental Precepts.' In the oral teaching and face-to-face transmission of our school as well, the precepts handed down from the West[5] are given to students; these are the Bodhisattva Precepts. However, in the preceptual scripture it says, 'recite this day and night.' Why have us abandon this recitation?"

Dogen said, "It is so; students should certainly observe the regulations of Pai Chang. However, their form is the receiving of precepts, observance of precepts, sitting meditation, and so forth. When it says to recite the preceptual scripture day and night and to wholeheartedly keep the precepts, it means that one should follow the practice of the Ancients and concentrate only on sitting. When sitting in meditation, what precept is not maintained? What merit is not produced? The practices carried out by the Ancients all had a profound intent. Without retaining your own subjective appreciation, you should follow the community and act in accord with the behavior of the Ancients."

3

ONE DAY HE SAID,

In the community of the meditation master Fo Ch'ao[1] there was a monk who wanted to eat meat when he was sick. Fo Ch'ao allowed him to eat it. One night the master himself went to the infirmary and looked in; there in the dim lamplight the monk was eating meat, while at the same time a demon was sitting on the sick monk's head eating that very same meat.[2] Though the monk thought it was going into his own mouth, it was the demon, not he himself, that was eating it. Henceforth, whenever a sick monk wanted to eat meat, the master knew he was possessed by a demon, so he allowed it.

As I reflect upon this, there should be due consideration as to whether or not to permit something. In the community of Wu Tsu Fa Yen[3] there were instances of eating meat. Whether permitting or forbidding, the attitudes of the Ancients all had to have had particular intent.

4

ONE DAY HE SAID,

Know that if a person is born in a particular House[1] and enters a particular path, he must above all cultivate the work appropriate to that House. If it is not your own path and you know it is not proper to your own station, it is wrong to cultivate it.

Now as men who have left home, when you enter the family of Buddha and become monks, you must practice the appropriate activity. To practice the appropriate activity and maintain the appropriate bearing means to abandon selfish clinging and follow the instructions of the teacher. The essential meaning of this is to have no greed or desire.

If you would be free of greed, first you must leave selfhood behind. In order to leave selfhood behind, the contemplation of impermanence is the foremost mental discipline.

Most worldly people want to be always well spoken of and well thought of by others. However, they are not always well spoken of, nor well thought of. If step by step you abandon selfish clinging and follow the words of your teacher, you will progress. If you claim to acknowledge this truth, yet, saying, "That may be so, but I can't abandon such and such a thing," if you cling to it fondly and practice it, you will sink lower and lower. The foremost mental discipline for a monk in order to improve is that he should concentrate only on sitting. It is not a question of cleverness or dullness, of sagacity or stupidity; if you sit in meditation you will naturally become good.

5

He instructed,

Extensive study and broad learning is something that cannot succeed. You should firmly resolve to give it up altogether. Only in respect to one task should you learn the ancient standards of mental discipline. Seek out the footsteps of past masters, wholeheartedly apply effort to one practice, and avoid any pretense of being a teacher of others or a past master.

6

Once ejo asked, "What is the principle of 'not being ignorant of cause and effect'?"[1]

Dogen said, "It is 'immutable cause and effect.'"

Ejo said, "How can one escape?"

Dogen said, "Cause and effect are clear."

Ejo said, "Then does cause evoke effect, or does effect evoke cause?"

Dogen said, "If it is so in every case, then take the example of Nan Ch'uan killing the cat:[2] when the assembly could not answer him, he immediately killed the cat. Later, when Chao Chou put his sandals on his head and went out, this was the acting out of yet another stage."

[Dogen also said,] "If I had been Nan Ch'uan, I would have said, 'Even if you can speak, I will kill it; and if you can't speak I will also kill it. Who quarrels over the cat? Who saves the cat?' In behalf of the community, I would say, 'We cannot speak; go ahead and kill the cat, teacher!' Or I would say in behalf of the community, 'The teacher only knows about one stroke cutting into two pieces; he does not know about one stroke cutting into one piece.'"

Ejo said, "What is one stroke cutting into one piece?"

Dogen said, "This is the cat itself." He also said, "When the assembly did not reply, if I were Nan Ch'uan I would say the assembly had already spoken, and would have released the cat.[3] An Ancient said, 'The Great Function appears without remaining in set patterns.'" He also said, "The 'cat' we are talking about is the manifestation of the Great Function of Buddha Dharma. And it is a 'turning word.'[4] If it were not a turning word, we could not say, 'Mountains, rivers, and the great earth, are the marvelous pure illumined mind'; and we could not say, 'The very mind is Buddha.' So in the expression of this turning word, see that the cat is identical to the Buddha-body. Furthermore, hearing these words, a student may suddenly become enlightened." He also said, "This cutting of the cat is just the activity of Buddha himself. What can you call it?" He said, "It must be called killing a cat."

Ejo asked, "Is this a form of wrongdoing, or not?"

Dogen said, "It is a form of wrongdoing."

Ejo said, "How to escape from it?"

Dogen said, "[The activity of Buddha and the wrongdoing] are separate, without appearing to be so."[5]

Ejo asked, "Does the term 'step by step liberation'[6] refer to something like this?"

Dogen said, "Yes. However, such considerations, even though they be a good thing, are not as good as no thing."

Ejo asked, "Does the expression 'violation of precepts' refer to transgression after having received the precepts? Or can a form of wrongdoing done before receiving the precepts also be called violation of the precepts? What about it?"

Dogen said, "The name of 'violation of precepts' should refer to transgression after having received the precepts. Wrongdoing which is done before receiving the precepts is just called a form of wrongdoing, wrong action; it should not be called 'violation of precepts.'"

Ejo asked, "In the forty-eight lesser precepts, I see that it refers to transgression even prior to receiving the precepts also as 'violation'; what about this?"

Dogen said, "It is not so. When one who has not yet received the precepts is about to receive them, as he repents of the wrongdoing he has committed, aspiring to these precepts, his transgression of the ten great precepts with which he was formerly invested, as well as his subsequent violation of the lesser precepts, is called 'violation of the precepts.' The wrongdoing he committed in the past is not called 'violation of precepts.'"

Ejo asked, "I read that now as he is about to receive the precepts, for the sake of repentance of wrongdoing formerly committed, one should teach the ten great and forty-eight lesser precepts to him who has yet to receive them, and should have him read and recite them. Yet in a subsequent passage it says that one should not explain the precepts to one who has not received them. What about the contradiction between these two points?"

Dogen replied, "'Receiving the precepts' and 'reciting the precepts' are different. To recite the preceptual scriptures for the purpose of repentance is also reading and contemplating the scripture. Therefore, one who has not yet been invested would recite the precepts. There can be no fault in explaining the preceptual scripture to him. The subsequent passage [which you mentioned] prohibits such an explanation to one who has not yet received the precepts, when it is done for the sake of profit. To one who is presently receiving the precepts, in order to have him repent, one should most certainly teach him the scripture."

Ejo asked, "Receiving the precepts is not permitted to those who have committed the seven grave wrongs.[7] In the former precepts, I read that even those guilty of grievous wrongs can repent. What about it?''

Dogen replied, ''Truly they should repent. When they are not permitted to receive the precepts, this is a temporary method of repression or curbing, meaning to put a stop to [their evil ways]. And the former sentence [means] that even if one has violated the precepts he is pure and clean; it is not the same as before receiving [the precepts].''

Ejo asked, ''Once repentance is permitted of the seven grievous wrongs, should they again receive the precepts?''

Dogen replied, ''Yes. This was the standard espoused by the late high priest Eisai himself: once repentance is allowed, then they should receive the precepts. Even if they are guilty of grievous wrongs, if they have remorse and want to accept the precepts, you should administer them. This applies all the more to Bodhisattvas, who should cause others to accept the precepts even at the risk of incurring fault in themselves.''[8]

7

IN AN EVENING TALK, HE SAID,

Do not use foul language to chastise and belittle monks. Even if it is an evil and incompetent person, do not scorn him or vilify him without consideration. In the first place, no matter how bad they may be, when more than four monks are assembled, this is the Community of Monks [Sangha] and is an important treasure of the nation. It should be most highly trusted and honored. Even if you are an Abbot, an Elder, even if you are a teacher, a wise man, if your disciples are out of line, you should teach and guide them with a compassionate heart, a kind heart.[1] At such a time, even if you strike those who need be struck, if you chastise those in need of chastisement, you should not allow feelings of depravation or vilification to arise.

When my late master Ju Ch'ing was abbot of T'ien T'ung, while the Community of Monks were sitting in meditation in the monks'

hall, in order to admonish them for sleeping, he would use his slipper
to hit them with, and chastise them with derogatory words; nevertheless, the Community of Monks were all glad to be beaten, and they
praised him.

One time in the course of his address he said, ''I am already advanced in age; by now I should have taken leave of the community
and should be dwelling in a hermitage caring for my old age. Nevertheless, as the teacher of the community, in order to shatter the
delusions of each of you, and to transmit the Way, I am acting as
Abbot. Therefore, I sometimes bring forth words of chastisement,
and I do things like beat you with a stick.[2] For this I have great trepi-
dation; nevertheless, it is the way to uphold the standard of the
Teaching in place of the Buddha. O brethren, please extend your
compassion to forgive me for this.''

When he had spoken thus, the Community of Monks all wept. It
is with just such a mind as this that one should handle the community and bring forth the Teaching. It is wrong to govern a community arbitrarily just because one is the Abbot and Elder, thinking
of them as belonging to oneself and chastising them. So, needless to
say, it is wrong to point out others' shortcomings and blame them
for their faults when you are not such a man yourself.

You should watch out very carefully: when you see the error of
another, if you think it is wrong and compassionately wish to guide
him, you should employ tact to avoid angering him, and should contrive to appear to be talking about something else.

8

HE ALSO TOLD A STORY, SAYING,

When the late General of the Right [Minamoto Yoritomo][1] was
first a captain of the Imperial Guard, once when he went out to attend an official party in the Imperial domain, there was a man there
who got out of order. At that time the grand privy councillor said to
Minamoto Yoritomo, ''You must restrain him.''

The general said, ''Someone should report it to Rokuhara; he is
the generalissimo of the Taira Clan.''[2]

The privy councillor said, "It's very near here, so [go ahead]."
The general said, "I am not the man to do it."

These are excellent words; with such a mind he later governed the land. Students of the present day should also have this mind; if you are not such a man yourself, do not criticize others.

9

IN AN EVENING TALK HE SAID,

In ancient times there was a general named Lu Chung-lien who subdued the enemies of the court in the land of the lord of Ping-yuan. Though the lord of Ping-yuan tried to reward him with much gold and silver and other things, Lu Chung-lien refused it all and said, "It is only because it is the way of a general to do so, that I attack the enemy well; it is not to obtain rewards or take things." So he said he dared not accept.

Lu Chung-lien is famous for his straightforwardness. Even in the ordinary world, those who are wise simply are what they are and accomplish their own way. They do not think of obtaining rewards. The mental attitude of students should also be like this. Having entered the Way of the Buddhas, carrying out various things for the sake of the Buddhist Teaching, you should not think there will be anything to gain in the way of reward. In all the inner [Buddhist] and outer [non-Buddhist] teachings, they only exhort us to be free from acquisitiveness.

10

AFTER A DISCOURSE ON THE TEACHING, HE SAID,

Even if one is speaking in accord with the truth, if another says something prejudicial, it is wrong to argue the point to defeat him. Then again, even though you consider yourself evidently correct, if you say it was your mistake and quickly retreat, this is too hasty.

It is best just not to pick others apart, nor to declare it one's own bias, but to be unconcerned and desist. If you act as though you hadn't heard and forget it, others will forget too and will not be angry. This is a most important point to be mindful of.

11

HE INSTRUCTED,

Impermanence is swift; the problem of life and death is a great one. While you are alive for the time being, if you practice some activity and are fond of study, you should only practice the Way of Buddhas and study the Teaching of Buddha. Because composition, poetry, and songs are worthless, it is right that you should abandon them. Even in studying the Buddhist Teaching and practicing the Buddha Way, still you should not study many things at once. So much the more should the Exoteric and Esoteric holy doctrines of the Scholastic schools[1] be completely put aside. You should not fondly study many of the words of even Buddhas and Patriarchs. Even when concentrating solely on one thing, people who are of inferior capacity with dull faculties cannot succeed. So how much the more is it unsuitable to try to do many things at once and have the tone of your mind out of harmony.

12

HE INSTRUCTED,

Of old, a man known as the meditation master Chih Chiao[1] aroused his will and abandoned his home in this wise: originally this master was a civil official. Endowed with intelligence and ability, he was an honest and upright wise man. When he was a provincial governor he stole government funds and gave them away. Others reported this to the emperor.

Upon hearing this, the emperor was greatly astonished, and all of his ministers thought it strange. The crime was not a minor one, and it was decided that capital punishment should be administered.

At this point the emperor discussed the matter, saying, "This minister is a man of talent, a wise and good man. Now he has purposely committed this crime; could it be that he has some deep motive? When you are about to behead him, if he shows any sign of grief or distress, behead him immediately: if he shows no such signs, then he must certainly have some deep intent, and you should not behead him."

When the imperial emissary brought him out to be beheaded, he showed no sign of distress; rather, his appearance was one of joy. He himself said, "I give this life to all sentient beings."

The emissary, surprised and struck with wonder, reported this to the emperor. The emperor said, "It is so; he certainly has some profound intent: I knew it had to be so." Therefore, he asked what his intention was.

The master said, "To leave public office, give up my life, practice charity, form a bond with all creatures, be born in a Buddhist family, and singlemindedly practice the Buddha Way."

The emperor was moved by this and allowed him to leave home. Therefore, he bestowed on him the name Yen Shou, "Prolonging Life," because he had stayed a certain execution.

Patchrobed monks of today should also once arouse such a mind; with a profound heart, which thinks little of your own life and has compassion for living beings, you should arouse a mind which aspires to entrust your bodily life to the Buddhist precepts. If you already have such a mind, even for a moment, you should preserve it so as not to lose it. Without once arousing such a mind, there can be no awakening to the Buddha Way.

13

IN AN EVENING TALK HE SAID,

The basis for understanding talk about Zen in the school of the Patriarchs is to take the mind which thinks it already knows, and revise it step by step in accordance with the words of the teacher.

Even if the manner of your original knowledge has been that you know Buddha to be Shakyamuni,[1] or Amida,[2] etc., replete with excellent characteristics[3] and radiant halo, possessed of the virtue of teaching Dharma and benefiting living beings, yet if the teacher should say that "Buddha" is a frog or a worm, you should believe that frogs and worms are Buddha, and should abandon your former understanding. If you look for the auspicious marks and radiant halo and the various merits of a Buddha on those worms, it means that your emotional views have still not changed. It is just a matter of knowing what one sees just then as Buddha. If in this way you go on revising your emotive views and original attachments in accordance with the teacher's words, then you will naturally come to an understanding.

However, students of recent times cling to their own emotive views and base themselves on their own opinions: thinking that Buddhahood must indeed be such and such a way, if it is something different from what they themselves think, they say it can't be that way; as long as they are wandering in delusion seeking something which resembles their own emotional judgements, most of them make no progress on the Buddha Way.

Again, having climbed to the top of a hundred foot pole[4] without sparing your bodily life, then when you are told to let go your hands and feet and advance one step further, you say that it is only when one has life that one can study the Buddhist Teaching; in reality this is not really obeying the teacher. You should consider this carefully.

14

In an evening talk he said,

Even worldly people, rather than study many things at once without really becoming accomplished in any of them, should just do one thing well and study enough to be able to do it even in the presence of others.

How much the more is this true of the supramundane Buddha Dharma: it is a way which since beginningless past has not been cultivated or practiced; and therefore, it is now still far from us. Our natures too are dull. In this exalted and far-reaching Buddha Dharma, if one takes on too many things at once, it will be impossible to perfect even one thing. Even concentrating solely on one thing, those whose faculties and capacity are dull by nature will have difficulty in thoroughly mastering it. Strive, students, to concentrate on one thing alone.

Ejo asked, "If so, then what thing, what practice in the Buddha Dharma, should we be solely devoted to cultivating?"

Dogen replied, "Although it should be in accord with potentiality and conform to capability, that which is now transmitted and solely practiced in the school of the Patriarchs is sitting meditation. This practice takes in all potentials and is a method which can be practiced by those of superior, middling, and inferior faculties alike.

"When I was in the community of my late master at T'ien T'ung monastery in China, after hearing this truth, while sitting still day and night, the monks thought in times of extreme heat or extreme cold that they would probably become sick; so they temporarily left off sitting. At that time I thought to myself, 'Even if I should become sick and die, still I should just practice this. If I fail to practice when I'm not sick, what is the use of treating this body tenderly? If I sicken and die, that is my will. To practice and die in the community of a master in the great country of China, and, having died, to be disposed of by a worthy monk, this would above all form an excellent affinity [for a good birth]. If I died in Japan, I couldn't be disposed of by such a man in accordance with the Buddhist ceremony, which is in conformity with Dharma. If I kept practicing and died before realizing enlightenment, from having established this affinity I should be born in a Buddhist family. If I do not practice, even if I maintained bodily life for a long time, it would be worthless. What would be the use? While my body is sound and I feel I will not fall ill, when unexpectedly I may drown in the ocean or meet an unforeseen death, how will I regret it afterwards?'

"I continued to deliberate in this manner, and being firmly resolved, as I sat upright day and night, I did not get sick at all. Now each of you should be thoroughly determined to practice and see; ten out of every ten of you should attain the Way. The exhortations of my late master at T'ien T'ung were like this."

15

He instructed,

People resolve to abandon even life, cutting off even their limbs and flesh, hands and feet; such acts are done in an insincere manner.[1] Therefore, thinking of worldly affairs, many make such resolutions because of a mind which grasps at fame and profit.

Just meeting situations as they arise, taking things as they come, is difficult. When a student is eager to abandon his bodily life, he should settle down for the moment and decide, in respect to what to say and what to do, whether it is in accord with the truth or whether it is not in accord with the truth: if it is in accord with truth, he should say it, and if it is in accord with truth, he should do it.

16

HE INSTRUCTED,

People who study the Way should not be anxious over food and clothing. Just preserve the Buddhist precepts and do not carry on worldly business. The Buddha said, "For clothing there are rags; for food there are alms." In what age would these two things ever be exhausted? Do not forget the swiftness of impermanence and trouble yourselves in vain over worldly things. While life, which is like dew, is temporarily here, think of the Way of Buddhas and do not be concerned with other things.

Someone asked, "Although the two paths of fame and fortune are difficult to abandon, because they are great hindrances to the practice of the Way, they should be abandoned. Therefore, I give them up. Although food and clothing are minor factors, yet they are of great importance to the wayfarer. The wearing of rags and begging of food is that which people of superior faculties practice; and it was the custom in India. In the monasteries of China there are things like the permanent temple endowment;[1] therefore, they have no problem in that respect. In the temples of our country there is no permanent endowment, and the custom of begging has also now died out and has not been transmitted. What can a body do whose faculties are inferior and incapable of endurance? To someone like me, then, even if I would covet the alms of a faithful patron, the fault of unworthy acceptance would come along with it. To be a farmer, merchant, warrior, or artisan would be gaining food by means of an improper way of life.[2] If one were to just leave it to fate, the result would still be poverty. When hunger and cold come, they would be distressing, and as such would hinder the practice of the Way.

"Some people criticize, saying, 'Your standards of behavior are extreme: you seem unaware of the times and blind to [people's] potentialities; they are of inferior faculties, and this is the Last Age.[3] If they were to practice in such a fashion, it would cause them to regress. It would be better to obtain the patronage of a donor or attach oneself to a lay supporter, take care of the body in a carefree and quiet dwelling place, and peacefully practice the Buddha Dharma with no worries about food or clothing. This is not greed for property or possessions; one should practice after having provided for temporal means of livelihood.'

"Although I hear these words, I cannot yet believe in or act upon them; what about such considerations?"

Dogen replied, "Just study the behavior of the patchrobed ones, the manner of Buddhas and Patriarchs. Although the three countries [India, China, and Japan] differ, those who genuinely study the Way never have such concerns. Just do not attach your mind to worldly affairs; you should wholeheartedly study the Way.

"The Buddha said, 'Other than robes and bowl, do not keep anything at all; what is left over from the food you have begged, you should give to hungry beings.' Even if you receive something, you should not store any up; how much less should you go to any trouble for the sake of food! In a non-Buddhist book it says, 'If you hear of the Way in the morning, it is all right to die that night.'[4] Even if we should die of starvation or die of cold, even for one day or one hour we should follow the Buddha's teaching.

"Over ten thousand aeons, a thousand lives—how many times will we be born, how many times die? All is because of arbitrary clinging to worldly entanglements. Following the Buddha's precepts for this one life, should we die of starvation, it would be eternal peace and comfort. But for that matter, I have never heard of a case in the whole canon of a single one of the traditional Buddhas and Patriarchs who died of starvation or died of cold. Mundane provision of food and clothing is a lot to which one is born, and does not come by seeking; and though one does not seek it, it is not that it is not forthcoming. Just resign yourself to fate and do not hold this in your heart. If you use the 'Last Age' as a pretext for not arousing the mind of the Way in this very life, then in which life will you find the Way?

"Even if you are not comparable to Subhuti[5] or Mahakashyapa,[6] you should just study the Way according to your capacity. In a secular writing it says, 'Even if it is not Hsi Shih or Mao Ch'iang, those who love the flesh love the flesh; even if it is not Flying Rabbit or Green Ears, those who love horses love a horse; even if it is not dragon liver or phoenix marrow, those who love flavor love flavor.'[7] It is just a matter of using as much wisdom as one has.

"Even some lay people have such standards; Buddhists should also be thus. How much more so since the Buddha has even turned over the endowment of twenty years[8] to us in the last age; because of this, for the monasteries of the world, the honor and support of humans and gods has not ceased. Although the Tathagata was abundantly blessed with metanormal powers and could use them freely, he spent a summer eating wheat horse fodder. Should not his disciples in the last age respectfully look up to this?"

The person asked, "Rather than falsely accept the offerings of men and gods while breaking the precepts, or vainly waste the endowment of the Tathagata without having a mind for the Way, how would it be to follow the lay people, perform the tasks of the lay life, and live for a long time to accomplish the practice of the Way?"

Dogen replied, "Who told you to violate precepts or to be without the mind for the Way? You should just forcibly arouse the mind which seeks the Way, and practice the Buddhist Teaching. Indeed, we read that the Tathagata's blessings are bestowed equally without discussion of keeping the precepts or violating the precepts, without discriminating between beginners and those with experience; but I have not seen it written that if one breaks the precepts he should return to lay life, or that without the mind of the Way one should not practice. Who possesses the mind of the Way from the very outset? If you just in this way arouse that which is difficult to arouse, and carry out that which is difficult to carry out, you will naturally progress.

"Everyone has the nature of a Buddha: do not foolishly demean yourself. Again, in the *Wen Hsuan*[9] it says, 'A country flourishes because of a single man; the former sages are set at naught by later fools.' What this means is that when a single wise man appears in a nation, that nation flourishes; if a single fool appears, the way of the sage is abandoned. Consider this.''

17

IN THE COURSE OF A TALK on various subjects, Dogen said,

Many men and women of the world, young and old, talk about sexual intercourse and such things. They use this to divert their minds, taking it for amusing conversation. Although it seems like entertaining the mind for a while and amusing oneself in a leisurely way, it is something to be absolutely avoided by monks. Even in the ordinary world, it is something that does not occur when good, earnest people, conscious of propriety, engage in serious discussion. It is the kind of conversation which takes place at times of drunkenness and debauchery.

How much more so for monks: they should think only of the Way of Buddhas. Miscellaneous talk is spoken by a few eccentric and disorderly monks. In the monasteries of China, since they do not indulge in miscellaneous conversation at all, of course they do not speak of such [erotic] things either.

Even in this country, when the high priest Eisai of Kennin Temple was alive, such kind of talk did not come up at all; even after his death, while a few of those were left who had been his disciples, they did not ever speak of such things. Recently, in the last seven or eight years, the young people appearing now are sometimes indulging in such conversation. It is a sorry state of affairs.

Even in the Sage's Teachings it says, "Coarse and violent evil acts can cause people to wake up: useless talk can obstruct the True Path." Even be they merely words spontaneously spoken, useless talk is a factor which hinders the Way; how much more so of [erotic] talk like this; drawn by the words, the mind will surely be immediately aroused. One must be most circumspect. Even if you do not consciously determine not to speak in such a way, once you realize it is a bad thing, you can overcome it gradually.

18

IN AN EVENING TALK, HE SAID,

Most people of the world, when they do something good, they want it to be known by others; when they do something bad, they do not want others to know: because of this, since such a frame of mind is not in accord with the minds of the unseen beings,[1] they experience no recompense for the good things they have done, and they receive punishment for the bad things which they have done in secret. Because of this they turn around and tell themselves that there is no result from good actions, and that there is little benefit in the Buddhist Teaching. This is a perverted view which should most certainly be revised.

Do good privately, while others are unaware; when you have made a mistake and gone wrong, afterwards reveal it and repent: if you act in such a way, then there will be reward experienced for the good you have done in secret, and having repented of the bad things which are revealed, the fault will be dissipated; therefore, there will naturally be manifest benefit even in the present, and you may be sure of future results.

A certain layman came and asked, "In recent times, whereas the laity make offerings to the Community of Monks, take refuge in and revere the Buddhist Teaching, due to the occurrence of much misfortune, wrong views have arisen and they are inclined not to take refuge in the Three Treasures. What about it?"

Dogen replied, "This is not the fault of the Community of Monks or the Buddhist Teachings; it is just the fault of the lay people themselves. The reason is that you give offerings to monks who maintain discipline of behavior and diet, even if it is just a matter of show; but when shameless monks who violate the precepts drink liquor and eat meat, you think it is improper and do not give them offerings. This discriminating attitude is in reality contrary to the intention of the Buddha. Therefore, the act of taking refuge and obeisance is void of merit, and there is no response. In the precepts too, various passages admonish this frame of mind. If it is a monk, you should make offerings to him whether he has virtue or not. In particular, one should not decide whether or not he has inner worth on the basis of his outward appearance.

"Although monks of the Last Age may outwardly appear to be distinguished in some way, yet there are wrong mental states and wrong actions which outweigh this. Therefore, without any thought of distinction between good monks or bad monks, if you make offerings and render them respect with an impartial mind just because they are disciples of Buddha, you will not fail to accord with the will of Buddha, and the benefits will be far-reaching.

"Furthermore, you should remember that there are the four expressions, 'hidden activity, hidden response; manifest activity, manifest response; [hidden activity, manifest response; manifest activity, hidden response].[2] Also there are the three periods of activity —reward in the present life, in the next life, and in succeeding lives. You should study these principles carefully.''

19

IN AN EVENING TALK, HE SAID,

When someone comes and discusses his affairs, if it should happen that he requests a letter,[1] perhaps to ask something of someone else, or perhaps to file a public suit, at that time, if you should refuse the request of the one before you, saying, 'I am not a worldly man:[2] because my station is that of a recluse who has left the world, it would be wrong for me to say something to a lay person which is not appropriate to my status,' although this seems to be the true way for one who is not a worldling, yet if we examine the inner state of mind there, if you do not comply because you are still thinking along such lines as 'I am one who has left the world; if I say something inappropriate to my status, people will surely think ill of me,' this is still selfish clinging to name and reputation.

Just take careful consideration when you are faced with such a situation; if it is something that should be of some benefit to the person who confronts you, then you should do it regardless of whether people will think ill of you. What is so bad about estrangement from a friend who is so lacking in understanding as to turn against you, saying 'This is improper; it is wrong'? Even though outwardly you may appear to others to be doing something partial and inappropriate to your status, the most important concern is to destroy selfish attachment and to abandon name and reputation. When people came to them and asked of them, the Buddhas and Bodhisattvas even cut off their bodies, flesh, hands, and feet. How much the more, then, when someone comes and asks for a single letter; to refuse that request, thinking only of your name and reputation, is deep attachment to self.

People are not sages: even if they think you are worthless, saying that you are someone who says things inappropriate to your status, still, if you abandon your own reputation to be of some help to others, you would be in conformity with the True Path. There are many instances in which the Ancients also appear to uphold this principle of conduct. I also take this principle into consideration. In a situation where someone asks you to communicate something rather unexpected to your patron or friends, it is easy to send a single letter and be a bit of help.

Ejo asked, "This matter is truly as you say: it is most reasonable to communicate a good thing that will be of benefit to someone. But in case someone wants to usurp another's possessions by some injustice or would say something detrimental to another, should one transmit the message?"

Dogen replied, "The matter of right or wrong is not for us to know. Just tell the other party, and also write in the letter, that although you have provided the letter because it was requested, he should deal with it in acccordance with right and wrong. It is the person who will receive and deal with it, who should determine whether it is right or wrong. In matters such as this, which are not our concern, it is also wrong to distort the truth in speaking of them to that person.

"Again, even though it be an obvious wrong, if there is someone who thinks highly of you and is such a friend that you would not go against whatever he said, good or bad, and he has an unacceptable request to make of your patron on biased grounds, even if you may assent to his request, in the letter you should write that you are only saying it because you can hardly refuse to do it, and that it should be decided upon in accordance with right and wrong. If you always do it this way, neither one will feel any resentment. In affairs such as this, when dealing with people face-to-face and in reference to matters that arise, you should make very careful consideration. The essential point is that in confronting situations you should give up attachments to name, reputation, and self."

20

IN AN EVENING TALK HE SAID,

In the present time, most people, both the worldlings and those who have left the world, are concerned that others know when they do something good, and hope that others do not know when they do something bad. Because of this, there develops a lack of harmony between inside and outside. Be sure to harmonize inside and outside, repenting of mistakes, hiding real virtue and not adorning outward appearance. One must maintain a spirit of attributing good things to others, while taking bad things upon oneself.

Someone asked, "To hide one's real virtue and not adorn one's outward appearance is truly the way it should be. However, the Buddhas and Bodhisattvas consider great compassion and the saving of beings to be fundamental: if ignorant monks and lay people should slander and criticize when they see that one's outward appearance is not good, they would incur blame for slandering the monks. Even if they are unaware of real virtue, if they respect, honor, and make offerings when they see the outward form, it should be a blessing. What about these considerations?"

Dogen replied, "If you just act in an unrestrained and dissolute manner on the pretext of not adorning your outer appearance, this is still contrary to what is right. To display bad behavior in the presence of householders or others, claiming that you are hiding your real virtues, this too is an extreme violation of discipline. Wishing to be known to others as one possessed to a rare degree of the mind of the Way, as a man of the Path, although you want others to be unaware of your own defects, yet this is something which all the gods, the benevolent spirits, and the Three Treasures secretly see and know. What is admonished here is the attitude which feels no shame on that account, yet wishes to be honored by worldly people.

"As you face the moment and meet the situation, you should just consider all things for the sake of the flourishing of the Teaching and for the benefit of living beings. After taking consideration, speak; after thinking, act: it means that one should not be wild. In all matters, you should determine what is right when you are confronted with them. Thought after thought does not linger; day after day flows away: the swiftness of impermanence is a fact right before our eyes. You need not wait for the teachings of a master or written scriptures; thought after thought, without making plans for the next day, thinking only of the present day, the present hour, since the days to come are extremely indefinite and impossible to know, you should only think of following the Way of Buddhas just for today, as long as you are alive. To follow the Way of Buddhas means to abandon bodily life and carry out various activities for the sake of the flourishing of the Teaching and the benefit of living beings.''

Someone asked, ''In following the Buddhist Teaching, should we practice begging for alms?''

Dogen replied, ''It should be so. However, there should be allowance made in accordance with the customs of the land. Whatever it may be, one should adopt whatever method there be whereby benefit to living beings may be far-reaching, and one's own practice also would progress.

''But by such a method as this [begging], where the streets are dirty, if one were to traverse them while wearing the Buddhist vestments, they would become soiled. Furthermore, the people are poor and house-to-house begging[1] would be inappropriate. It seems that the practice of the Way might regress, and the benefits would not be far-reaching. If we just observe the customs of the land and continue to practice the Way in a forthright manner, the high and low will give offerings of their own accord; both personal practice and the teaching of others will be accomplished.

''In such matters, too, one must consider what is right in view of the time and circumstances, unconcerned with the views of others. Forgetting one's personal profit, one should strive to do what will promote the Way of Buddhas and the benefit of living beings.''

21

He instructed,

Regarding the fact that students of the Way must abandon worldly feelings, there are several levels to be mindful of: they are to abandon the world, abandon home, abandon the body, and abandon the mind. You should consider them well.

Although they have fled society and dwell hidden in the mountains and forests, there are those who do not break with their family, which has continued generation after generation, and they still think of their families and relatives.

Again, although one flee society, abandon home, and go far from the land of one's relations, when one thinks of his own body, determined not to do anything painful, disdaining to carry out something which may give rise to illness, even though it be the Way of Buddhas, he has still not abandoned his body.

Again, although one carries out difficult and painful practices without anxiety for his body, as long as his mind has not entered the Way of Buddhas and he refuses to do what is contrary to his own inclinations, even though it be the Way of Buddhas, he has not abandoned his mind.

NOTES TO 1

1. Compiled by Tao Hsuan (595–667), prodigious author and founder of the South Mountain Sect of the Vinaya (Lu), or discipline sect in China, based on the four-part books of discipline.
2. Sanskrit *sharira*; purple crystals found in the cremation ashes of a Buddha. These were supposedly often found in the ashes of great Buddhists in China and Japan, and enshrined in stupas.
3. Japanese *Nyorai*; one of the epithets of a Buddha. Literally, the Sanskrit means (one who has) Thus Come, or Thus Gone. The Japanese, via Chinese, chooses the former.
4. Sanskrit *Mara*; the Tempter.
5. The Three Jewels, or Treasures, are Buddha, Dharma (his Teaching), and Sangha (the Community of Followers).
6. Japanese *shikan taza*; "only sitting." This is one of the most important terms of Soto Zen; it means sitting meditation without any specific object of concentration, such as the *koan*. Dogen's teacher Ju Ch'ing had emphasized pure sitting as superior to all other practices.

NOTES TO 2

1. Japanese *noso*. The word *no* means patching or mending, and it also means robe, specifically the robe of a Buddhist monk. In the early days of Buddhism, Shakyamuni and his followers used to wear garments made of rags sewn together. Later, when Buddhism had become an established religion, monks often took to wearing fine robes presented by the faithful. The Zen monks, however, generally known as the most frugal and austere of early Buddhists in China and Japan, referred

to themselves as "patchrobed monks," identifying themselves with the ancient tradition of poverty and simplicity.

2. Myoan Eisai (1141-1215), usually referred to by Dogen as the late *Sojo*, or "high priest" of Kennin Temple, journeyed to China twice. The first time he went with the idea of revitalizing the decadent Tendai School; on his second trip, which lasted five years, he received the teaching of the Huang-Lung line of Lin Chi Ch'an (Rinzai Zen). Back in Japan, he founded the Kennin Temple in Kyoto, where he taught the so-called "Three Teachings"—Tendai, Shingon (esoteric Buddhism), and Zen. Thus, he is known as the founder of Rinzai Zen in Japan. Dogen first studied Zen under Eisai's pupil Myozen, and has naught but praise for Eisai himself, though he scorned that latter's posterity for their rapprochement with secular powers, and their luxurious living habits.

3. The *Bonmokyo* (Brahmajala-sutra) contains the so-called "Bodhisattva Precepts," or "Fundamental Precepts," consisting of ten great and forty-eight lesser precepts. It is thought to have been composed in China.

4. Pai Chang Huai Hai (720-814), a great Chinese master, is said to have put together "pure rules" (*ch'ing kuei*) for the organization and conduct of specialist Zen monasteries; the earliest extant codification, said to be based on Pai Chang's work, dates from the eleventh century.

5. In the Zen tradition, the transmission from the West is usually taken to refer to Bodhidharma, the legendary founder of the sect who came from India to China in the fifth or sixth century. Since Buddhism as a whole came to Japan via China and Korea, it is all a transmission "from the West."

NOTES TO 3

1. Honorific title of Cho An Te Kung (1144-1203). This story is not found in the Choenji text of the *Zuimonki*.

2. That the demon represents the sickness is clear from what follows.

3. Wu Tsu Fa Yen (? -1104) was a great master of Lin Chi Ch'an. He did not leave the householding life until the age of thirty-five. According to *Eihei Dogen Chiji Shingi,* after he had penetrated Zen, his master sent him to be a miller at the foot of the mountain where the monastery was; he was accused of drinking wine, eating meat, and keeping ladies. When he heard of this, Fa Yen kept meat and wine around, and flirted with women customers whenever Zen students were around. Later it was discovered that he had secretly put three hundred thousand pieces of cash into the communal temple stores, which he had earned from his various business activities.

NOTE TO 4

1. A "House" or "Family" connotes a specialty, or walk of life.

NOTES TO 6

1. This expression is taken from a famous story about Pai Chang Huai Hai. Once an old man who used to attend Pai Chang's lectures, told him that in the distant past someone had asked him whether or not one who cultivates the great practice still falls into cause and effect. The old man had replied that such a one would not fall into the province of cause and effect; because of this reply, he became a "wild fox" for five hundred lives. Then he asked Pai Chang to save him from this condition, and posed the question to him as to whether or not one who cultivates

the great practice still falls into cause and effect. Pai Chang said, "He is not ignorant of cause and effect." The old man was then enlightened. The full story appears in example II of the collection *Wu Men Kuan* (*Mumonkan*), which is available in several English translations.

2. This incident also appears in the *Wu Men Kuan* (example XIV): once, when the monks of the eastern and western halls in his temple were arguing over a "cat," Nan Ch'uan grabbed the cat, held it up before them, and said, "If anyone in the community can speak, you will save the cat; if you cannot speak, I will kill the cat." No one spoke, so he killed the cat. Later, Nan Ch'uan's great disciple Chao Chou returned to the temple, and Nan Ch'uan related this incident to him. Chao Chou immediately put his sandals upon his head and walked out. Nan Ch'uan said, "If you had been here, you would have saved the cat." Nan Ch'uan P'u Yuan (748–834) and Chao Chou Ts'ung Shen (778–897) were both outstanding Chinese Zen masters.

3. This reading follows the Choenji text; the *rufubon* has it, "I would have said, 'The assembly cannot speak,' and would (not) have let the cat go." The former text has *hoge-semashi*, whereas the latter has *hoge-shitemaji*; in the latter, the *nigori* may have been improperly added, in which case the proper reading would be *hoge-shitemashi*, making it positive instead of negative in meaning.

4. A "turning word" epitomizes the revolution from delusion to enlightenment. In Zen texts it is used to refer to the answer to a problem, or to an expression of the teaching.

5. This is a difficult passage; the Choenji text has it, "They are separate (different), but both contained (in the act)." Evidently it means that killing the cat as an act of Buddha (to teach) and killing the cat as a form of wrongdoing are separate, or different, yet contained in the same outward appearance.

6. Sanskrit *pratimoksha,* "aimed at liberation." Precepts are recited out of context in the fortnightly *uposatha* ceremony, each one governing a distinct aspect of discipline, aimed at liberation. Each monk is supposed to examine his conduct in respect to each point raised. The act of killing the cat as a form of wrongdoing is distinct from the act as the act of Buddha in respect to the relation of the participants, just as one's relation to one's deeds is different after actually repenting or turning away, even though the deed in itself is the same.

7. The seven grievous wrongs, or "seven perversions" are (1) shedding the blood of a Buddha, (2) killing one's father, (3) killing one's mother, (4) killing one's teacher, (5) killing one's instructor, (6) disrupting the Community of Monks which strives to turn the Wheel of Dharma, and (7) killing a sage. The bad results of these deeds are experienced immediately.

8. The putative fault of the Bodhisattva would be that of transmitting the precepts to someone who appears unworthy.

NOTES TO 7

1. Literally, the heart of an old woman; a Zen expression for kindness and compassion.
2. *Chu pi* (*shippei*), a bamboo stick used for beating.

NOTES TO 8

1. Minamoto Yoritomo (1147–1199) fought against the Taira Clan and became the Shogun, or supreme military commander in Japan in 1185. He set up his capital in Kamakura, ushering in what is known as the Kamakura Era (1185–1334).

2. Rokuhara, in Kyoto, was the headquarters of the Taira Clan, military rivals of the Minamoto Clan; in 1160, Taira no Kiyomori (1118–1181) had himself appointed Shogun, and played a dominant role in Kyoto politics.

NOTE TO 11

1. This refers to the Tendai and Shingon schools, respectively.

NOTE TO 12

1. Yung Ming Yen Shou (904–975) became a successor in the third generation to the Fa Yen sect of Chinese Zen. He was the author of *Tsung Ching Lu,* a prodigious compilation of 100 scrolls of essays and quotations from Buddhist and Zen texts.

NOTES TO 13

1. Shakyamuni, the "sage of the Shakya clan," is an epithet of the historical Buddha Gautama.
2. Amida is a transhistorical Buddha, the object of devotion of the Pure Land schools of Buddhism. He is said to reside in the western direction, in a land called Sukhavati, "Abode of Happiness."
3. Buddhas (and all great men according to Indian tradition) are said to possess thirty-two auspicious marks, plus eighty minor excellent characteristics.
4. Ch'ang Sha Ching Ts'en, a distinguished disciple of Nan Ch'uan (see notes to book I, section 6), once composed the following verse:

> The man immobile atop a Hundred Foot Pole—
> Though he has attained Entry, this is not yet real.
> Atop the Hundred Foot Pole, one must advance—
> The universe in the ten directions is the Whole Body.

This is found in *Ching Te Chuan Teng Lu,* vol. 10.

NOTE TO 15

1. One way in which Gautama Buddha himself is said to have defined the Middle Way was to practice neither self-indulgence nor self-mortification, since both of these revolve around the concept of an individual self. In Chinese records there are to be found cases of voluntary dismemberment and self-immolation. The point which Dogen makes is that such acts are insincere when they become objects of pride or show: hence the "abandonment" is incomplete, no matter how dramatic the show. That is why Dogen says the student should restrain his impulses and decide what to do on the basis of truth.

NOTES TO 16

1. Permanent temple endowment, or, literally, "ever-abiding goods" refers to the real estate and other property of a temple; this was not "owned" by anyone, but was community property, of which personal use was forbidden. That this institution did not exist in Japan is an astonishing statement, inasmuch as the temples were great landowners. Probably it refers to the newly introduced Zen sect, specifically Dogen's community, which was subject to oppression from the old established sects, and, as is quite clear from this book, experienced great poverty and lack.
2. The four ways of life enumerated here are the Confucian description of society, representing for the Buddhists the secular life. The Zen monasteries of China

engaged in agriculture and business, but Dogen's outlook in these matters was extremely pristine and pure, perhaps because of the extreme degeneracy of the Japanese Buddhist institutions of his time.

3. The idea of three periods of the Dharma—True, Semblance, and Final—evolved some time after the death of the historical Buddha. The first two are generally supposed to last five hundred years each, while the Last Age, the degenerate age, would last as long as ten thousand years. The eras are described not simply in terms of the state of the Buddhist teaching, but in terms of the human condition.

4. This is quoted from the Confucian Analects (*Lun Yu*) IV, 8.

5. Subhuti was one of the Buddha's ten great disciples, known for his excellent understanding of emptiness.

6. Mahakashyapa, another of the Buddha's ten great disciples, was known for his great austerity, and is traditionally recognized as the second Patriarch (after the Buddha himself) of Zen.

7. Hsi Shih and Mao Ch'iang were exemplary beauties among women; "Flying Rabbit" and "Green Ears" were famous steeds.

8. Out of an idealized life span of one hundred years, Shakyamuni Buddha actually lived only eighty years: traditionally it is said that he bequeathed the remaining twenty years to his disciples.

9. The *Wen Hsuan* is an anthology of classical Chinese literature; Dogen has studied it in youth, and quotes from it a number of times in this text.

NOTES TO 18

1. These represent forces in the total makeup of cause and effect, which are not apparent or explicable; sometimes they are spoken of as the deities of Hinduism or Shinto, which came to be thought of as protectors of Buddhism.

2. The last two sets are to be understood; the text gives "etc."

NOTES TO 19

1. Inasmuch as monks were presumably literate; in Japan as elsewhere, monks often performed clerical tasks for the secular world.

2. Literally, "not a human being"—a *hinin,* or "outcaste."

NOTE TO 20

1. The standard practice followed by Buddha and his disciples was to beg at seven successive houses each time, regardless of whether a house were rich or poor.

BOOK II

1

HE INSTRUCTED,

If the wayfarer first just subdues his mind, it will be easy to abandon his body and the world as well. But if he thinks of others' views in respect to his speech and behavior, and refrains from doing something because people would think ill of it as a bad thing, or if he tries to do good when the opportunity arises, because if he did this thing others would look upon him as a true Buddhist, these are still worldly feelings. But if one, therefore, selfishly follows his own will and does bad things, he is a wholly evil man.

The point is to forget evil intention, forget one's own body, and just act wholly for the sake of the Buddha-Way. One must be mindful in all events.

For beginners in practice, even though they be worldly feelings, though they be human feelings, to subdue evil in the mind and practice good in the body, is none other than abandonment of body and mind.

2

HE INSTRUCTED,

When the late high priest Eisai was in Kennin Temple, a poor man once came alone and said, "My family is so poor that we have had no food for several days.[1] Husband, wife, and child, we are on the verge of starvation. Please have compassion and save us."

At that time there was no clothing, food, or goods in the temple at all. As Eisai thought of what to do, he came to a dead end. At the time there was a little bit of beaten bronze to be used for the halo in the construction of a statue of Yakushi Buddha:[2] this Eisai took and broke it off himself; rolling it up into a ball, he gave it to the

28

poor man and said, "You can exchange this for food to stave off
starvation."

That layman rejoiced and left. At the time Eisai's disciples criticized him; they said, "This was supposed to be the halo of an image
of a Buddha; what about the wrongdoing involved in making personal use of the Buddha's goods?"[3]

The high priest said, "That is truly so. But if we consider the
Buddha's own will, the Buddha cut off his flesh and limbs and gave
them to living beings. To living beings who are right now about to
starve to death, even to give them the whole body of Buddha still
would be in accord with the will of Buddha." He also said, "Even if
I were to fall into evil ways because of this wrongdoing, still I should
save living beings from starvation."

The loftiness of mind of the past master should be considered by
students of today as well. Do not forget it.

Another time, some disciples of the high priest Eisai said, "The
rooms of the Kennin Temple are near the river bed. In later times
there may be flooding."

Eisai said, "We should not think of the disappearance of our
monastery in future generations. Even of the Jetavana Monastery[4]
only the foundation stone is left. Nevertheless, the accomplishment
of having built the monastery is not lost; and for the time being, im-
measureably great would be the meritorious accomplishment of one
year or a half a year of carrying on the Way."

Now, as I think about this, since the building of a monastery is a
great task of a lifetime, one might also think about how to avoid
calamity even in the future; nevertheless, even in that frame of
mind, one should reflect upon the loftiness of mind which thought
along such lines [as Eisai].

3

In an evening talk, he said,

In the time of Emperor T'ai-tsung[1] of T'ang [his minister] Wei
Cheng said to him, "The people are slandering the emperor."

The emperor said, "If the sovereign has humanity, he should not
worry that people revile him; if he lacks humanity, he should worry
if he is praised by others."

Even a worldling was like this; monks should have such a mind above all. When one has compassion and has the mind of the Way, it is not of any consequence to be criticized and reviled by ignorant people. But if you lack the mind for the Way, to be thought of by others as possessing the Way, is something to be wary of.

Emperor Wen of Sui² said, "Secretly cultivate virtue, await fulfillment." What this intends to say is to practice good virtues, awaiting fulfillment, treating the common people with tenderness.³ If a monk has not yet attained to this, he should pay utmost heed. If one just inwardly cultivates the work of the Way, the virtues of the Way will appear outwardly of their own accord: without expecting or hoping to be known to others, if one singlemindedly goes along with the Teachings of the Buddha and follows the way of the Patriarchs, people will naturally be drawn to his virtue.

The mistake that has arisen among students here is that they consider the respect of others and the forthcoming of property and riches to be the manifestations of virtue; and other people also know that and think so too. Knowing in your heart that this is the affectation of the demons of temptation, you should be most deliberate. In the Teachings this is called the doing of demons. I have never heard, among the examples of the three countries, that one should regard material wealth and the reverence of the ignorant as virtues of the Way. Those who were said to have the mind of the Way from ancient times in the three countries were all poor and suffered bodily pain: frugal in all things, possessed of compassion, imbued with the Way, they were said to be people of genuine practice.

What is to be called the manifestation of virtue does not refer to abundance of material wealth and pride in offerings received. There must be three levels in the manifestation of virtue. First is that it be known that such a man is practicing such a way. Next is that people aspire to that way. Afterwards, they likewise study and likewise practice that way; this is called the manifestation of virtue.

4

IN AN EVENING TALK, HE SAID,

People who study the Way must abandon human emotions. What is called abandonment of human emotions is to go in accord with the

Way of Buddhas. People of the world are mostly possessed of the nature of the Lesser Vehicle: discriminating good and bad, distinguishing right and wrong, taking right and discarding wrong—this is all in the nature of the Lesser Vehicle.

One must only first abandon worldly emotions and enter into the Way of Buddhas. To enter into the Way of Buddhas is to abandon the act of distinguishing good and bad in your own mind, cease thinking "good" or "bad," forget conscious thoughts about the welfare of your own body or about the condition of your mental state, whether good or bad, and follow the speech and behavior of the Buddhas and Patriarchs. What you think in your own mind to be good, or what people of the world think is good, is not necessarily good. Therefore, forget the views of others, abandon even your own mind, and follow the Teachings of Buddha.

Even though your body be painful and your mind in distress, be resolved because you are one who has utterly abandoned his own body and mind; even if it be painful and likely to cause distress, if it was the practice of the Buddhas and Patriarchs, of the virtuous ones of days gone by, you should carry it out. Even though you think a certain thing may be good and should be in accord with the Way of Buddhas, though you wish to perform and carry it out, if it is something not included in the practice[1] of the Buddhas and Patriarchs, you should not do it. Thus, you will not fail to have understood the Teachings as well.

This is to abandon contemplation in your own mind of the doctrines you have originally learned, and just gradually shift your mind over to the words and behavior of the Patriarchal teachers[2] which you are now reading. If you do so, your wisdom will advance and your understanding open up. If there is a reason you should abandon what you have gained from the words of the Doctrinal school, which you have been originally studying, then you should abandon it and see from the point of view of this present meaning.

If you still are thinking deep inside, "The fundamental purpose of the study of the Teachings is for finding the path to liberation; how could I lightly abandon the accomplishment of many years of study?": then this mind is called a mind which is bound by birth and death. You should contemplate this thoroughly.

5

IN AN EVENING TALK, HE SAID,

The biography of the late high priest Eisai of Kennin Temple was written by the lay Buddhist[1] councillor of the middle rank Akigane. In his [first] refusal at the time, he said, "Let it be written by a Confucian. The reason for that is that Confucians forget their bodies from the beginning and from youth to maturity take up scholarship as their fundamental concern. Therefore, there are no errors in what they write. Ordinary people are essentially concerned with their own employment and social relations; since they take up scholarship as a sideline, even though they be personally good, mistakes occur in the course of their writing."

As I think of this, the fact is that people of ancient times forgot their bodies to study even in learning the Outside [non-Buddhist] Classics.

The late high priest Koin said, "What we call the mind of the Way means taking such a doctrine as 'Three thousand worlds in an instant of thought,'[2] studying it, encompassing and holding it within your breast; this is called the mind of the Way. To pointlessly wander around lost with a rainhat hung around your neck, is called the action of the deluding influence of pride."[3]

6

IN AN EVENING TALK HE SAID,

The late high priest Eisai has said, "The things such as food and clothing which everyone in the community uses, do not think that I give them to you. All of it is what is offered by various gods.[1] I have just distributed it as I got it. And you are each fully provided with your one-time span of life; so do not run around in haste. Do not think of gratitude to me." Thus did he ever admonish. I consider these to be most excellent words.

Also, the assembly of the Chinese meditation master Hung Chih[2] at T'ien T'ung monastery had provisions sufficient for a thousand people. There were thus enough provisions stored for seven hundred in the halls[3] and three hundred outside the halls;[4] but because a great Elder [Hung Chih] was living there, monks came from all directions like clouds, so that there were a thousand people in the halls and five or six hundred people outside. One of the directors of affairs petitioned Hung Chih, saying, ''The monastery provisions are sufficient for a thousand people; but crowds of monks have gathered, and there is not enough to go around. Could we deviate from the norm and turn some of them away?''

When he had said this, Hung Chih said, ''Everyone has a mouth; it is not your concern. Do not worry about it.''

Now as I think about this, everyone gets the food and clothing which is his lot in life: it does not come by taking thought for it, and it is not that it won't come if you do not seek it. Even householding people leave it to fate, thinking of loyalty and cultivating filial piety.[5] How then could leavers of home concern themselves with extraneous matters? There is the endowment bequeathed by Shakyamuni, there is the food and clothing offered by the gods to the worthy. And there is also the natural lot of life which we have by birth. Even without seeking it or thinking about it, just leaving it to fate, one must have his lot in life. Even if you pursue and obtain riches, what happens when impermanence suddenly arrives? Therefore, students should just study the Way wholeheartedly, without keeping other things on their minds.

Someone said, ''For the flourishing of the Buddhist Teaching in the Last Age in this outlying region,[6] if we contrive to dwell at ease in a quiet place, without worry about things like food and clothing because of outside support, and practice the Way of Buddha with food and clothing fully provided, the benefit should be widespread.'' Now in my opinion, this is not so. For that matter, as long as people who maintain appearances and are attached to self gather together to study, among them there would not appear a single one with an awakened mind. Attached to profit, addicted to desire for wealth, even if a thousand or ten thousand were gathered together, it would still be worse than if there were none at all. Only the active causes of evil dispositions would pile up of themselves; it is because of the lack of the spirit of the Buddhist Teaching.

If one is pure and poor, suffering hardship, sometimes begging for food, sometimes eating wild fruits, studying the Way in constant hunger, it is when someone hearing of this comes and wishes to learn that I feel he is a true bearer of the mind of the Way, and that is the flourishing of the Buddhist Teaching. If there be no one because of the hardship and poverty, or if there be many people gathered with an abundance of food and clothing but lacking in the Buddhist Way, these two are eight ounces and a half a pound.[7]

People of the present age generally regard the activities of constructing images and building pagodas as the flourishing of Buddhism. This too is wrong. Even with lofty halls adorned with polished jade and beaten gold, there could be no one who would attain the Way because of these. This is just a portion of merit, incorporating the wealth of householders into the Buddhist world to do good. Although it happens that they also experience a great result from a small cause, for monks to be occupied with such affairs is not the flourishing of Buddhism. Even in a grass hut or under a tree, pondering even a single phrase of the Teaching, practicing a single period of sitting meditation, this is indeed the true flourishing of Buddhism.

The fact that I am now soliciting contributions and working as much as I can to establish a monks' hall,[8] I do not necessarily consider to be the flourishing of Buddhism. It is just that for the time being, while there is no one to study the Way and I pass the days and months without purpose, I think that it is better [to do this] than to be idle; it may provide an opportunity for the deluded [to become enlightened], and it will serve the purpose of a place to sit in meditation for the seekers of the Way in the present age. Still, there should be no regret even if a thing conceived and begun is not completed: if even one pillar is set up, I do not care if in the future they shall see that someone had conceived of such an undertaking but could not complete it.

7

SOME PEOPLE EXHORTED DOGEN to go to eastern Japan for the propagation of Buddhism.[1] He replied,

"No. If someone had an aspiration for the Buddhist Teaching, he would cross mountains, rivers, and seas to come and study it. Even if I were to go to exhort people without that aspiration, it is uncertain as to whether they would listen. Would I just be fooling people for my own material support? Would it be because of greed for wealth? Because that is distressing to the body, my feeling is to let it be.''

8

HE ALSO SAID,

People who study the Way should not read the books of the Scholastic [Buddhist] schools, nor study the Outside [Non-Buddhist] Classics. If you must read, read the recorded sayings [of the Zen Patriarchs] and the like. As for the rest, you should put them away for the time being.

Meditating monks of recent times are fond of literary things, to compose verses and write sermons; this is wrong. Even without expressing it in verse, one may write what he thinks; though the literary style may not be polished, one may write down the teachings. A person who is so lacking in the mind of the Way that he would refuse to read it because it is crude, would only delight in words and would fail to grasp the principle even if there were exquisitely clever phrases in a highly polished literary style.

Since this is something that I had originally studied fondly since childhood, even now from time to time beautiful phrases from the Outer Classics occur to me, and things like the *Wen Hsuan* also appear to me; yet because I consider it to be pointless, I think that in fact it should be utterly abandoned.

9

ONE DAY HE SAID,

While I was in China, once when I was in a meditation cloister reading records of sayings of the Ancients, a certain monk from Ssu Ch'uan who was a Man of the Way asked me, ''What is the use of reading the recorded sayings?''

I answered, "So that I would know the behavior of the Ancients."
The monk said, "What is the use of that?"
I said, "To return to my native land and teach others."
The monk said, "What is the use of that?"
I said, "It is to benefit the living."
The monk said, "After all, what is the use?"

As I later decided what the truth was here, to read the recorded sayings, the public cases, and so forth, thus knowing the acts of the Ancients, or to speak of them for the edification of those who are deluded, all of this is ultimately of no use to one's own practice or the guidance of others.

Devoted solely to sitting, once you have illumined the Great Matter, then afterwards, even if you do not know a single letter, in elucidating and pointing it out to others, it can never be exhausted. For this reason did that monk say, "Ultimately, what is the use?" Thinking that this is the real truth, I subsequently gave up reading the recorded sayings and the rest; totally concentrating on sitting, I was able to clarify the Great Matter.

10

IN AN EVENING TALK, HE SAID,

Without real inner virtue, one should not be esteemed by others. Since people in this country esteem others on the basis of outer appearances, without knowing anything about real inner virtue, students who lack the mind of the Way are thus dragged down into evil ways, and become subject to temptation. It is easy to be esteemed by others. To put on a shallow pretence of having abandoned one's status[1] and turned away from society, is merely a fabrication of outer appearance.

While simply having the appearance of an ordinary person of the world, one who goes on harmonizing the inner mind is a genuine aspirant to the Way. Therefore has an Ancient said, "Inside empty, outside accords." What this means is to have no selfish thought in the inner mind, while the outer appearance goes along with others.

If one utterly forgets such things as "my body" and "my mind," and enters into the Way of Buddhas, acts in accord with the standards of the Buddhist Way, inside and outside are both good, now and afterwards are both good.

Even in the Way of Buddhas, it is wrong to rashly abandon that which is not to be abandoned, with the intention of abandoning one's self or abandoning the world. Among those in this country who pose as Buddhists and devotees of the Way too, he who acts badly for no reason, in the name of abandoning the self, without regard to how others may see him, or, in the name of non-attachment to the world, does such things as walk in the drenching rain, in spite of the fact that it is both inwardly and outwardly useless to do such things, people of the world immediately think what a venerable man he is, how detached from the world he is, and so forth. In their midst, if one observes the regulations of the Buddha, heeds the standards of discipline, and carries out his own practice and the conversion of others in accord with the Buddha's regulations, people will paradoxically say he smells of [greed for] fame and profit, and will have nothing to do with him. But that, on the other hand, for oneself is following the Buddha's Teachings and perfecting inner and outer virtue.

11

IN AN EVENING TALK, HE SAID,

Students of the Way, it is useless to be known to people of the world as a wise or knowledgeable man. But when there is even one person who is really and truly seeking the Way, one should not fail to explain what one knows of the Teaching of the Buddhas and Patriarchs. Even if it is someone who has tried to kill you, if he asks with a sincere heart, seeking to hear of the True Way, you should forget feelings of enmity and explain it for him. Beyond that, it is completely useless to pretend to know about things like the Exoteric and Esoteric as well as the Inner and Outer Classics. If someone should come and ask about these things, there would be nothing wrong at all in replying that you don't know. If you are troubled because others will think it bad to be ignorant, and you yourself feel like a stupid man, and so, in order to learn things, you study widely the Inner and Outer Classics, and furthermore fondly study many things so as to know about the worldly concerns of ordinary people, or else pretend to others to be knowledgeable, this is a serious mistake. It is really useless for the study of the Way.

Even if you pretend not to know what you do know, since this is strained and artificial, it is after all an affront, and it is wrong. There is nothing wrong with not knowing in the first place.

When I was a child I enjoyed and studied things like the Outer Classics. Subsequently, even till I went to China and received the Dharma, I opened up the Inner and Outer Classics, even so far as to become fluent in the local language; an important task, it was something exceptional even in the worldly way. Even the lay people considered this extraordinary: and even though it was in one respect a necessary task, as I now consider fully, it happened to be a hindrance to the study of the Way.

But even if you read the Teachings of the sages, if you go on gradually imbibing the principles you read in the writings, you should grasp their meaning. However, you look first at the literary style, watch for parallel phrases and rhyming sounds, think to yourselves "this is good, this is bad," and only afterwards embrace the principles. Therefore it were better to go on from the very beginning to imbibe the principles without knowing so much.

In writing talks on the Teaching as well, if you try to express it in literary style, thinking that if the sound harmony is off, it would be a hindrance, this is the fault of knowing. Let the language and style be as they may; if one would record the principles one by one as he thinks of them, even if those who come afterwards may think the phraseology is poor, as long as the principle comes across, it is important for the work of the Way.

Other talent and learning is also thus. Tradition says that the late Ku-Amidabu was originally a great scholar of the Exoteric [Tendai] and Esoteric [Shingon] schools. After he abandoned the world, after he had entered the gate of Buddha-remembrance,[1] it happened that there was a teacher of Shingon who came and asked about the doctrines of the Esoteric school: at that time, Ku-Amidabu answered him, "I have forgotten them all; I do not remember a single letter." Thus, in effect he did not answer. Just such as this should be the model of the mind of the Way. It seems he must have had some recollection; but the fact was that he did not say anything useless. It seems that the way of thoroughgoing remembrance of Buddha must indeed be like that.

Students today should also have such a mind. Even if you already have talent and learning of the Doctrinal schools, it would be a good thing to forget all of it. Needless to say, you should certainly not study them now. Even the recorded sayings of our [Zen] sect should not be read by one who is truly engrossed in study. As for the rest, it should be obvious from this.

12

IN AN EVENING TALK, HE SAID,

At the present time, people of this country, whether in respect to speech or in respect to behavior, mostly think of good and bad, right and wrong, in terms of the seeing, hearing, consciousness, and knowledge of worldly people: "If I do that, others will think it bad; if I do this, others will think it good"—in this way they cling, even into the future.

This is totally wrong. People of the world cannot necessarily be considered good. However people think, let them think so; let them even call you a madman: in your own mind do that which would accord with the Way of Buddhas, and refrain from doing that which does not conform to the Buddhist Teaching. If you pass your whole life in this way, it is of no consequence how people of the world may think.

To "flee the world" means that one does not let the feelings of worldly people hang on his mind. If you just study the actions of the Buddhas and Patriarchs, learn the compassion of the Bodhisattvas, repent in the hidden presence of all the heavenly beings and benevolent spirits, and go on the Way by acting in deference to the regulations of the Buddha, you should have no trouble at all.

It is also wrong to be shameless before other people, to indulge in doing what is bad, on the grounds that it doesn't matter if people say or think it is bad. You should just act in total reliance upon the Buddhist Teaching without depending upon the views of other people. In the Buddhist Teaching too, such indulgence and shamelessness is restrained.

13

HE ALSO SAID,

Even in the manners of the mundane world, even if you are in a dark room or in a place where others cannot see you, even when changing clothes and sitting and lying down as well, to carelessly fail to conceal the private parts, lacking a sense of propriety, is censured as shamelessness before celestial beings and demons. Just conceal those places which are to be concealed, just the same as when others can see, and be ashamed of that which is shameful.

In the Buddhist Teaching also, the prohibitions and precepts are also like this. Therefore, one on the Way does not speak of inside or outside, does not choose between light or darkness; mindful in his heart of the Buddha's regulations, one should not do what is bad just because no one will see or know.

14

ONE DAY A STUDENT ASKED, "Although I have occupied my mind with the study of the Way for months and years, yet I have attained no measure of intuitive enlightenment. Many of the Ancients said that the Way does not depend upon intelligence or brilliance, and does not require one to have knowledge or acumen. Thus, I understand that I should not demean myself just because I have inferior faculties and poor capacity. Is there perhaps an ancient standard for a way of concentration that I can keep in mind?"

Dogen said, "Yes. Without use of knowledge or talent, not to depend upon brilliance or intellect, is true study of the Way. Yet it is wrong to urge people to misguidedly become like blind and deaf ignoramuses.

"Because the study of the Way does not use great learning or gifted abilities at all, no one should be despised as having inferior faculties or poor capacities. Sincere study of the Way should be easy. Yet even in the monasteries of the great country of China, among several hundreds or a thousand people gathered under one teacher, those who truly find the Way and obtain the truth are but one or two persons. Therefore, there must be some ancient standard for concentration.

"Now as I consider what this is, it is a matter of whether one's determination is thoroughgoing or not. People who arouse a true and genuine aspiration and engross themselves in study to the full extent of their capacity, do not fail to attain. As for the description of the essential point to be mindful of, what thing must be concentrated upon, what practice is to be considered most urgent, that is as follows.

"First is only that the aspiration of joyful longing be earnest. For example, suppose a person has a conscious desire to steal a precious jewel, a desire to defeat a powerful enemy, or a desire to embrace a distinguished beauty; while traveling, abiding, sitting, and reclining, in the midst of affairs as they pass, though various different events come up, he goes along seeking an opening, his mind occupied [with his quest]. With this mind so forcefully earnest, there can be no failure of attainment.

"In this way, when the aspiration to seek the Way has become sincere, either during the period of sole concentration on sitting, or when dealing with illustrative example of the people of olden times, or when meeting the teacher, when one acts with true aspiration, though [his aim] be high he can hit it, though it be deep he can fish it out.

"Unless you arouse a mind comparable to this, how will you accomplish the great task of the Buddha-Way, which cuts off the turning round of birth and death in a single instant of thought? If someone has such a mind, we do not talk about whether he has inferior wisdom or degenerate faculties, we do not discuss whether he is a stupid and ignorant evil man; he will definitely attain enlightenment. And to arouse this determination, it is necessary to earnestly contemplate the impermanence of the world.

"This task is not something which is to be considered as a temporarily prescribed method of contemplation. And it is not that you should invent something non-existent to think about. It is the truth in reality right before our eyes.

"One ought not depend upon the instruction of others, the words of the Sagely Teaching, or the inner principle of witnessing the Way. Born in the morning, dead at night; the fact that people we saw yesterday do not exist today is something that meets the eye everywhere and is close about the ears. This is something one sees and hears in respect to others: as one applies it to his own bodily self and considers what is true, even if one may expect a life of seventy or eighty years, in accordance with the truth that one must eventually die, one does die.

"During that interval, amidst its sorrows and joys, gratitude and love, resentment and enmity, and so forth, if one succeeds as he wishes, he may have passed the time in anyway at all. But only believing in the Way of Buddhas, one should seek the true bliss of nirvana. How much the more so for people grown old, people whose lives are half gone; since the remaining years can only be so many, can you be lax in studying the Way?

"Yet even this truth is put off to the future. In actual reality it is this day, this moment, that one should think of the things of the world and of the things of the Way of Buddhas; tonight or tomorrow, you may contract any kind of disease, with such oppressive physical pain that you cannot distinguish east from west; or you may incur enmity and injury from some kind of demons or spirits and may die suddenly—you may meet some kind of trouble with brigands, or enemies may appear and you may be killed, wounded, deprived of life. It is truly uncertain.

"Therefore, in a world of such troubles as these, to deliberate upon various means of livelihood in order that one may extend one's life as far as possible—in spite of the fact that the time of death is completely uncertain—and besides this to even plot evil towards others, to pass the time in vain, these are acts which are foolish in the extreme.

"It is just because this principle is really true, that the Buddha himself spoke of it to the masses of living beings; and in the general teachings and talks on the Way of the Patriarchal teachers as well, this principle alone is expressed. In our gatherings in the Teaching Hall and requests for instruction also, it is customary to say, 'Impermanence is swift; the matter of life and death is a great one.'

"Returning to it again and again, without forgetting this principle in the mind, just thinking for this day, this time only, without losing a moment, you should put your mind into the study of the Way. After that it is really and truly easy. As for natural superiority or inferiority, or the sharpness or dullness of faculties, they are not to be discussed at all.''

15

IN AN EVENING TALK, HE SAID,

The fact that most people do not flee the world appears as if they were attached to their own bodies; but the fact is that they are not thinking of their own bodies. This means that they have no foresight. Also, it is because of failure to meet a good teacher.

Even if one hopes for gain and sustenance, if one does obtain the benefit of eternal bliss, even if one wishes to have the offerings of dragons and celestial beings, and considers name and repute, if one does attain honor as a Buddha or Patriarch and obtain the epithet of an Ancient Worthy, wise people in later generations should respect and look up to it when they hear of it.

16

IN AN EVENING TALK, HE SAID,

An Ancient said, "Having heard the Way in the morning, one may well die that night."[1]

Now people studying the Way should also have such a mind. Over a period of vast aeons and many lives, where you have been born in vain and have died in vain so many times, when you have, by a rare chance, gotten a human body and happened to encounter the Teaching of the Buddhas, if you don't rescue this body now, in what lifetime will you rescue this body? Even if you look after and maintain the body, you could not succeed. Since life must eventually be left behind, if one would abandon even a day or an hour of it for the sake of the Buddha's Teaching, it would be a basis for eternal aeons of bliss.

While thinking about what is to come, about livelihood for tomorrow, if one does not abandon the world which must be abandoned, does not travel the path which is to be traveled, and thus passes the days and nights in vain, this is a matter for regret. One must simply resolve that if there be no means of livelihood tomorrow, then may he die of starvation, may he die of the cold, but he must above all arouse the mind which, even for today, this one day, having heard the Way, would die if that were in accord with the will of a Buddha. In this case, it is certain that one will be able to attain the Way.

Without this mind, even though it may seem like you have turned away from the world and are studying the Way, if you are still holding back, and keep such matters as summer and winter clothing on your mind, thinking of maintaining life tomorrow and even next year, if you try to study the Buddhist Teaching in this way, even if you study for ten thousand aeons, in a thousand lifetimes, I don't think you would succeed.

Yet maybe there could be such a person. But according to what I know, it doesn't seem to me that this could be the Teaching of Buddhas and Patriarchs.

17

IN AN EVENING TALK, HE SAID,

Students should think of the fact that they will surely die: this truth is indisputable. But even if you do not think about that fact, you should, for the time being, determine not to pass the time in vain; you should not spend time in vain by doing useless things, but by doing things which are worthwhile should you pass the time.

Among those things which are to be done, today, which of all things is most important? Know that everything outside of the actions of Buddhas and Patriarchs is all useless.

18

EJO ONCE ASKED, "In the activity of a patchrobed monk, if one mends and patches old and worn-out clothing and such without throwing them away, it seems as if he is greedy in being sparing of things. Yet if he discards the old and uses the new accordingly, he has a mind which is greedy in seeking what is new. There being fault in either case, ultimately how should one deal with this?"

Dogen replied, "If one just detaches from both greed in sparing and greed in seeking, there would be no impropriety in either case. However, would it not be appropriate to mend what is worn, making it last a long time, and not to covet anything new?''

19

AFTER AN EVENING TALK, EJO ASKED, ''Should we perform such duties as the requital of the debt of gratitude to our fathers and mothers?''

Dogen answered, ''Filial piety and obedience are most certainly to be exercised. However, in that filiality and obedience there is a difference between householders and leavers of home.

''Householders observe such Teachings as those of the *Classic of Filial Piety* [*Hsiao Ching*], serving [their parents] in life and serving them in death; worldly people all know this.

''Because leavers of home abandon the debt of gratitude and enter into non-doing, in the manner of a leaver of home, when it comes to requital of debt, it is not limited to one person; thinking with deep gratitude of all sentient beings alike as fathers and mothers, he returns the roots of goodness he creates back to the universe. If one were to limit it specially to his parents in this life's single generation alone, he would go against the path of non-doing.

''In daily practice of the Way, continuous immersion in the study, if one just goes on following the Way of Buddhas, that is to be considered the true way of filial piety. The dedication of offerings on death anniversaries and the practice of good during the period of limbo are activities which lay people resort to.

''The patchrobed ones should know the depth of their debt to their fathers and mothers such as it truly is. And you should know that everything else is also like this. To specially divine a day to practice virtue, or especially choose one person to whom to dedicate it, does not seem to be the intention of the Buddha. As for the passage in the preceptual scripture about the day of death of father, mother, and siblings, this seems to be temporarily applied to householders. In the monasteries of China, although they have such ceremonies on the death anniversary of the master, it doesn't appear that they practice this on the death anniversaries of parents.''

20

ONE DAY HE SAID,

A person is said to have dull faculties when his determination is not thoroughgoing. When a worldly person falls from a horse, even before he hits the ground, various thoughts arise. When something happens that is so serious that one will injure his body or lose his life, anybody would use what intelligence he has by nature or by learning, to think [what to do]. At such a time, those of sharp faculties and those of dull faculties alike think of things and decide what is right.

Therefore, thinking that one may die tonight or die tomorrow, forming the idea that one is in a hopeless situation, in earnestly driving his determination on, one cannot fail to realize enlightenment. Rather than being superficially clever in worldly wisdom, it is the one who seems to be of dull faculties, yet who arouses a sincere determination, who quickly attains enlightenment. That the likes of Cudapanthaka,[1] who lived when the Buddha was in the world: even though he could hardly recite even a single verse, because his root nature was earnest, he obtained realization in the course of one summer retreat.

Our lives are only here for now. As long as you study the Buddhist Teaching with the earnest intent to obtain awakening before you die, there should not be a single person who would fail to attain.

21

ONE EVENING HE SAID,

In the meditation cloisters of China, it happens that they sift their wheat and rice and such, getting rid of the bad and taking the good, making it into cooked rice or whatever.

A certain meditation teacher criticized this in a verse, saying, "Even though your head be broken into seven pieces, do not sift the rice." His meaning was that monks should not arrange vegetarian meals or the like; depending on what there is, they should eat the food when it is good, and when it is bad, they should eat it without disgust. It is just a matter of using the faithful donations of patrons and the pure and clean food from the temple provisions to ward off hunger and support life to practice the Way. It means that one should not choose between good and bad on the basis of taste. The members of my congregation now should also have such a mind.

22

As someone asked, "If a student, hearing that one's own self is the Buddha-Way and that one should not seek outside, would deeply believe in these words, abandon his former practice and study, and spend his lifetime doing good or evil deeds according to his basic nature, how is this understanding?"

Dogen said, "In this understanding, the words and the principle are contradictory. If, on the premise that one should not seek outwardly, you abandon practice and leave off study, it seems like there is something sought by this practice which is abandoned. This is not non-seeking.

"Just realize that practice and study are fundamentally the Buddha-Way itself; without any object of seeking, even if in your heart you want to do things like the evil deeds of the world, do not do them, and do not weary or take notice of the boredom of the practical exercise of the study of the Way: on the basis of this practice, cultivating it singlemindedly, it is when you carry on without any quest from your own mind, even as to fulfilling the Way or obtaining the result, that you would be in conformity with the principle that you should not seek outwardly.

"Nan Yueh's 'polishing a tile to make a mirror' also was admonishing Ma Tsu's quest to become a Buddha.[1] It is not that he proscribed sitting meditation. Sitting is itself the act of a Buddha; sitting is itself non-doing. This is just one's own true body. The thing is that you should not seek a special way to enlightenment beyond this."

23

One day after private instruction, he said,

Many monks of recent times say that one should go along with worldly customs. Now as I consider this matter, it is not so. Even in the mundane world, the wise say that it is impure to follow the vulgar ways of the populace. Take the likes of Ch'u Yuan,[1] declaring that "All the world is drunk; I alone am sober," he did not go along with the ways of the people, and in the end drowned in the Ts'ang river. How much the more so in the Buddhist practices is everything contrary to worldly actions. Lay people adorn their hair; monks shave their hair off. Lay people eat a lot; monks eat once a day. Everything is contrary. Afterwards, though, they become people of great peace and bliss; therefore do monks turn away from the habits of the world.

24

ONE DAY HE SAID,

In the method of governing the world, from the emperor above to the multitudes of people below, all of those who occupy specific offices cultivate the appropriate work. When those who are not suitable are occupying office, that is called rebelling against heaven.

When the course of government is in harmony with the inner will of heaven, the world is tranquil and the people are at ease. Therefore, the emperor arises in the third quarter of the third watch [about half past two A.M.], making that the time for the government of the land. It is not an easy thing.

As for the methods of Buddha, it is just a matter of a change of station and difference of work. The king of a nation by himself uses his intellect to plan the course of government, considering former guidelines, seeking ministers endowed with knowledge of the Way; when the affairs of government and the will of heaven are in mutual harmony, this is called governing the world. If this is neglected, heaven is rejected, the world is in confusion, and the people suffer.

From there on down, all the various dukes, nobles, officers, knights, and common people each have the work which they do. To follow this is called humanity. To go against this confuses the affairs of heaven, and therefore is subject to the punishment of heaven.

Therefore, you people who study the Way of Buddhas should never for a single moment wish to rest your bodies idly on the pretext of detachment from society and of having left the householding life. Although at first it seems to have benefit, later on it would be greatly detrimental. Following the manners of leavers of home, you should completely master this station and carry out its tasks.

In the government of the mundane world, though they consider precedent and seek the worthy, if there are no examples handed down by former sages and past masters, then it even happens that they would follow the example of the times on their own; but for Buddhists, there are definite precedents and written teachings right before us. Also, teachers who bear the accepted tradition presently exist.[1]

I have a thought. In all phases of comportment, if in every respect you consider former guidelines and follow past masters in cultivating your practice, how could you fail to attain the Way?

Lay people want to be in accord with the will of heaven; patch-robed ones want to be in accord with the will of Buddha. They carry out their tasks equally, but the [latter] result obtained is superior; once attained, it is attained forever. For the sake of such great tranquility and joy, to suffer one generation of illusory transformation, this body, to follow the will of Buddhas, should alone be in the heart of the wayfarer.

Nevertheless, there is nothing in the Buddhist Teachings which encourages anyone to rashly torment the body or do things which are not to be done. If you go in accord with the practice of restraint and the refinements of behavior, your body will naturally be at ease, your behavior consistent and unobtrusive to others. Therefore, abandoning the selfish ideas of bodily comfort which you are now entertaining, you should acquiesce completely to the Buddha's regulations.

25

HE ALSO SAID,

When I was studying in the meditation cloister of T'ien T'ung in China, the Elder Ju-ch'ing used to sit in meditation until about half past eleven at night, and rose in the morning from about half past two to sit in meditation. We sat together with the Elder in the monks' hall. There was no relaxing even for one night.

During that time, many monks fell asleep. The Elder walked around hitting sleeping monks with his fist, sometimes taking off his slipper to strike them with, shaming and exhorting them, awakening them from their sleep. If they still slept, he would go to the Hall of Illumination and ring the bell, call the servants to light the lamps, and give an impromptu general talk, such as:

"Since you have gathered in a monks' hall, what is the use of idly sleeping? Why then have you left your homes and entered a monastery? Have you not seen the sovereigns and officials of the world— who among them takes life easy? The lord masters the Kingly Way and the ministers fulfill loyalty and integrity, and so on down to the peasants, who cultivate the fields, wielding the hoe: who passes easily through the world? Having entered a monastery to avoid all this, if you pass the time in vain, after all, what will be the use? The matter of life and death is a great one; impermanence is swift: the doctrinal schools and the meditation schools alike exhort us in this way. Tonight, tomorrow, one may meet any kind of death; one may suffer any kind of illness. As long as you are alive for the time being, it is foolish not to carry out the Way of Buddha, instead of passing the time in vain by lying down and sleeping. It is for this reason that the Buddhist Teaching is declining. When the Buddhist Teaching was flourishing everywhere, in all the monasteries they concentrated on sitting in meditation. In recent times, because they do not encourage sitting meditation everywhere, the Buddhist Teaching is running thin."

I saw with my own eyes how he admonished the congregation of monks with such reasoning, and made them sit and meditate. Students of the present day too should think about his manner.

Also, one time his attendants who waited on him close by said to him, "The monks in the monks' hall are sleepy and tired, and may become sick, or their wills may flag. Perhaps this may be due to the long period of sitting: how would it be to shorten the time period for sitting meditation?"

The Elder was very indignant; he said, "It should not be so. When those who lack the mind of the Way tarry idly in a monks' hall, even were it for just a little while, they would still fall asleep. If they have the mind of the Way and a will to accomplish its practice, the longer the time the more they would rejoice in cultivating it.

"When I was young, as I traveled to see the Elders of various regions, a certain Elder admonished me in this fashion: 'Previously I would beat sleeping monks so hard my fist would almost break; but now I am old and my strength is faded, so that since I cannot beat them hard, no more good monks appear. It is because the Elders of the various regions are lax in encouraging sitting meditation that the Buddha's Teaching has declined. I should hit harder.'"

26

HE ALSO SAID,

Is the Way attained by means of the mind, or by means of the body? In the Scholastic schools they say that body and mind are identical; though they say that the Path is attained by way of the body, yet they say it is because of this identity. Therefore, the fact that it is truly the attainment of the body is not made clear.

Now in our school, both body and mind attain together. Between them, as long as you use your mind to judge and compare the Buddhist Teachings, you will never attain it in ten thousand aeons in a thousand lifetimes. When you let go of your mind and abandon knowledge and understanding, that is when you attain.

Cases like "Seeing form, illuminating the mind; hearing sound, awakening to the Way;[1] are also the attainment of the body. Therefore, if you completely abandon the thoughts and views of the mind and simply sit, the Path will be found near at hand. Thus, the attainment of the Way is accomplished by means of the body. Therefore, it is my feeling and advice that you should concentrate on sitting alone.

NOTES TO 2

1. Literally, "no smoke (in the hearth)"; nothing to cook.
2. Sanskrit Bhaishajyaguru, Buddha of medicine and healing.
3. That is, personal use of community property of the Sangha.

4. This refers to the vihara in the Jetavana grove in India, bought by Anathapindika from a Prince Jeta, it was given to Shakyamuni Buddha and his followers. Thus, it is a most ancient and famous site of Buddha's teaching, in modern day Oudh (ancient Kosala).

NOTES TO 3

1. The second emperor of the T'ang dynasty, T'ai Tsung lived from 598 to 649, and reigned from 627 to 649. Even today he is recognized as a great emperor. He is said to have admonished his ministers that for a ruler to squeeze and exploit his people was just like gouging out his own flesh to eat.
2. Founder of the Sui Dynasty, Emperor Wen lived from 541 to 604, and reigned from 589 to 604. His greatest feat is to have unified China after centuries of political division and strife. He was exemplary in his frugality, encouraging the livelihood of the peasants by land allotment, and restricting government spending.
3. *Itsukushu suru:* this means to have compassion for, to treat tenderly, or to make upright; according to Dogen's line of thinking represented here, these meanings are virtually synonymous.

NOTES TO 4

1. The Choenji text gives, "not in the heart of the Buddhas and Patriarchs."
2. This refers to the Zen records, based on the words and deeds of the masters, rather than the theories and doctrines of the intellectual or Doctrinal schools which had hitherto been studied by Buddhist scholars in Japan.

NOTES TO 5

1. *Nyudo:* literally, one who enters the Way; this refers to lay people who take the tonsure and accept the basic Buddhist precepts. Sometimes called "lay monks," this was a very popular institution among the Japanese aristocracy.
2. This is a formula of the Tendai school, representing the highest perception of their Teachings. The three thousand worlds represent all times and all conditions of existence; to embrace them all in a single mental instant is the highest meditative attainment of the Tendai school.
3. *Tengu,* or "heavenly dog," has the vernacular meaning of a braggart; it is a long-nosed creature which dwells in the mountains—the long nose associates it with pride. Wandering around with a rainhat hung round the neck refers to one making a living by means of his appearance as a monk, without really having the mind of the Way, thus arrogating monkhood to his own self.

NOTES TO 6

1. Gods are conceived of as beings who enjoy wealth and power and all earthly delights; thus it can be used as a polite way of referring to rich people.
2. Hung Chih Cheng Chiao (1091–1157) was an outstanding master of Ts'ao-Tung, or Soto Zen, the sect which Dogen transmitted to Japan. His *Tso-ch'an Chen,* "Guide to Sitting Meditation," was highly regarded by Dogen, who considered it the finest work ever written on the subject; Dogen's own paraphrase of it is contained in the *Shobogenzo,* 27.
3. Meditating monks.
4. Temple workers; the great Sixth Patriarch of Zen, Hui Neng, had been such a worker rather than a monk when he was in the community of the Fifth Patriarch.

5. Loyalty and filial piety were cardinal Confucian virtues, means of advancement in a Confucian utopia.
6. Japan is here referred to as an "outlying area" in respect to China and India, classical centers of Buddhist culture.
7. That is to say, "six of one and a half-dozen of the other."
8. A monks' hall is also referred to as a meditation hall; it is a special institution of the Zen communities.

NOTE TO 7

1. Kanto, eastern Japan, was where the military government was seated in Dogen's time. In those days, as today, many teachers of philosophy and religion resort to the ruling class as an obvious source of support. In particular, a number of Zen teachers came to Japan from China in the thirteenth century and received protection and support from the military establishment at Kamakura; as refugees (from the Mongols), however, their circumstances were somewhat special. Dogen's teacher Ju-ch'ing had warned him to stay away from rulers of men.

NOTE TO 10

1. Or, "body": in this case I have chosen "status" since this reflects the custom of the time of nobles and officials "abandoning" secular affairs and taking Buddhist orders. Often, however, this was to the advantage of political maneuvering or decadent living.

NOTE TO 11

1. *Nembutsu;* this refers to the practice of the Pure Land schools of reciting the name of Amida Buddha. Although the man concerned was already ordained, he is said to have "abandoned the world" (*tonsei*) when he entered the Pure Land Way because he gave up the status of a great scholar of the established powerful schools, to live in retirement and devote himself to recitation of the Buddha's name.

NOTE TO 16

1. *Lun Yu* IV, 8. This is probably the saying of Confucious which is most frequently quoted in Zen circles.

NOTE TO 20

1. Cudapanthaka, one of the Buddha's disciples, is representative of the most ignorant and stupid. Unable to remember any phrases of the Teaching, he was given a broom by the Buddha; by concentrating on this, eventually he attained liberation.

NOTE TO 22

1. Huai Jang of Nan Yueh (677–744) visited his future disciple Ma Tsu Tao I (709–788) and found the latter sitting constantly in meditation. Nan Yueh asked him, "What are you striving for by sitting in meditation?" Ma Tsu said, "I am striving to become a Buddha." Nan Yueh then picked up a piece of tile and began to rub it on a rock. Ma Tsu asked him what he was doing, and he said, "I am polishing the tile to make a mirror." Ma Tsu asked, "How can you polish a tile to make a mirror?" Nan Yueh said, "Granted that polishing a tile will not make it a mirror, how can sitting in meditation produce a Buddha?"

NOTE TO 23

1. Ch'u Yuan (289?-243? B.C.) was a statesman during the Warring States period in ancient China. He was from Ch'u, now corresponding to central China, but then a southern area of Chinese civilization. Accused in an intrigue and exiled south of the Yangtse River, he wrote the famous *Ch'u Tz'u,* "Elegies of Ch'u," eulogizing the beauties of his homeland and lamenting the political troubles of his time. Eventually, he cast himself in the Mi Lo River (not the Ts'ang, as Dogen relates).

NOTE TO 24

1. It is evident that Dogen considered himself among their number.

NOTE TO 26

1. This famous slogan is based on the enlightenment of two ninth-century masters, Ling Yun Chih Chin and Hsiang Yen Chih Hsien; both had studied for a long time with the famous teacher Kuei Shan Ling You, but attained nothing. One day Chih Chin saw some peach blossoms and was immediately enlightened. Chih Hsien went to live by the abandoned tomb of an ancient master; one day as he was sweeping the area, a piece of tile he swept hit a bamboo trunk, and when he heard the noise, Chih Hsien awakened to the Way.

BOOK III

1

HE INSTRUCTED,

Those who study the Path must let go of mind and body and enter wholly into the Way of the Buddha. An Ancient said, "Atop a hundred foot pole, how will you step forward?"[1] Thus, having climbed to the top of a hundred foot pole, there is a mind which thinks that it will die if it lets go its foothold, and so holds fast. The admonition to take a step forward means that having concluded that it would not be bad, then, so as to cast off body and life, one must deliberately abandon everything, from his worldly occupations to his lifetime career. As long as he does not abandon this, no matter if he studies the Way with the same urgency as of beating out a fire on his head, it would still be impossible to attain the Way. You must settle your resolve and cast off body and mind together.

2

ONCE A CERTAIN NUN ASKED, "Even worldly women strive to study for the Buddhist teaching. As for a nun, even though there may be slight imperfection in her person, I do not know why she should not be fit for the Buddhist Teaching. What about it?"

Dogen said, "This interpretation is wrong. Although it happens that lay women do study the Buddha's Teaching while remaining as they are, and do have some attainment, if a person who has left home does not have the heart of a leaver of home, she cannot attain.

"It is not that the Buddha's Teaching chooses among people; it is because people do not enter into the Buddhist Teaching. The standards and mentalities of leavers of home and householders must be different. If a householder has the heart of a leaver of home, he can escape; for a leaver of home to have the heart of a householder is a double fault.

"The fact is that the approaches must be much different. It is not that the doing is difficult; it is that it is difficult to do well. Because in spite of the fact that the journey of escape to find the Way seems to be on everyone's mind, those who really accomplish it are rare.

"The matter of life and death is great; impermanence is swift. Do not relax your mind. If you abandon the world, you must abandon it truly. As for temporarily established names, let them be what they may."

3

IN AN EVENING TALK, HE SAID,

As I look upon the people of society in the present time, those people who obtain good results and promote their families are all upright and straightforward of mind, and are benefactors of others. Therefore, they maintain their homes and flourish even through their children and grandchildren.

As for people who are crooked in their minds and malevolent toward others, even if for a day it seems their results are good and their homes maintained, eventually they turn out badly. Or even if they appear to pass their whole lifetimes without trouble, their posterity will inevitably decline.

Also, when doing good for others, if one does it with the wish to be well thought of and well liked by that person, this may seem better when compared to evil, but it is still thinking of oneself and is not really good for others.

Even though it be unknown to them, one who does what is good for others, even for the future, though not thinking of whose may be the benefit, who provisionally does what would be good for the sake of others, is called a truly good person.

All the more should a ragged monk uphold a mind which surpasses even this. His consideration of sentient beings does not distinguish between familiars and strangers; maintaining a will to help them equally, even though he does not think of his own profit at all, of mundane or transcendental benefits, and is neither known nor liked by others; he simply does in his heart what is good for others, and is not himself known by others to possess such a mind.

The rule for this is that one must first abandon the world and abandon one's own body. If one just truly abandons his body, he has no mind to wish to be well thought of by others. If, however, you say 'let the people think what they may,' and then do bad things, indulging yourself, this also goes against the will of the Buddha.

Just do what is good, carry out good deeds for the sake of others without thinking of obtaining a reward or of glorifying your name; being truly without possession, work for the benefit of living beings.

Thus, the most essential point to concentrate on is to detach from yourself. If you would maintain this mind, first you must contemplate impermanence. A lifetime is like a dream; time passes swiftly by. Dewlike life rapidly vanishes. Since time has never waited for anyone, as long as you are alive for the time being, you should think of being good to others, even in respect to the slightest matters, in accordance with the will of the Buddhas.

4

IN AN EVENING TALK, HE SAID,

People who study the Way must be utterly poor. As I see the people of the world, for those who have wealth, the two problems of anger and shame are sure to arise.

When one has a treasure, when he thinks that others will steal it, and he determines that it will not be taken from him, anger suddenly arises. Or perhaps in discussing this, when it comes to dialogue and settlement, eventually it creates a conflict and they engage in battle. While it goes on this way, anger rises and disgrace too befalls.

When one is poor and covets nothing, he has already avoided these problems and is free and at ease. The proof is right before your eyes; don't wait to find it in the scriptures.

What is more, the ancient sages and past worthies criticized it, and all the gods, the Buddhas, and Patriarchs, all put it to shame, when foolish people, nevertheless, store up property and treasure, and embosom so much anger and hatred; this is the shame of shames.

To be poor yet think of the Way is what the past worthies and ancient sages looked up to; it is that over which all the Buddhas and Patriarchs rejoiced.

The degeneration of Buddhism in recent times is right before our eyes. From the time I first entered and saw Kennin Temple, till the time when I saw it seven or eight years later, the things that had gradually changed were that they had put lacquered storage chests in each room, and each individual had his own utensils; taking a liking to fine clothing, they accumulated material possessions and indulged in rude talk: by reflecting upon the decline of such things as salutation and ceremonial obeisance, the state of other places can be inferred from this.

Buddhists should not possess anything at all besides robes and bowl. What is there to put in it that one might need to make a lacquered chest? One should not have so much that he hides it from others. It is just because of fear of thieves that one thinks of hiding things away; if one abandons them and does not hold on to them, he will then be at ease. It is only when one thinks he will not be killed by others even though he must kill then, that the body suffers and the mind is worried: if one has determined that even if people kill him, he would not retaliate, then one's mind is not worried and he does not trouble about thieves. One would never be ill at ease.

5

ONE DAY HE SAID,

When the Zen master Hai Men was Great Elder at T'en T'ong, there was a monk in his congregation known as Senior Yuan.[1] This man was one who had grasped the truth and awakened to the Way; his practice and attainment excelled even that of the Elder.

One night he went to the abbot's quarters, burned incense, bowed, and said, "Please allow me the head seat of the rear hall."[2]

At that time the Zen master wept and said, "Since the time I was a novice, I have never heard such a thing as this. For you, a meditating monk, to seek the head seat, or the position of Great Elder, is a serious mistake. You have already awakened to the Way better than I have. But is your seeking for the head seat for the sake of advancement? If I were to allow you, you could be allowed even the front hall³ or the position of Great Elder. Your attitude is base and ignoble; from this indeed can be inferred that of the other monks, who are not yet enlightened. The decline of the Buddhist Teaching can be known by this." So saying, he shed tears and wept sadly.

Although he deferred in shame at this, still eventually he was asked to occupy the head seat. Afterwards, the Senior Yuan recorded this talk, shaming himself and bringing his teacher's excellent words to light. As I consider this, the Ancients thought it shameful to seek advancement or to want to be the head of something or to be the Great Elder. Just think of awakening to the Path; there should be nothing else of concern.

6

ONE EVENING HE SAID,

After Emperor T'ai Tsung of the T'ang dynasty assumed the throne, he dwelt in the old palace. Because it was ruined, there was a dampness in the air, and the chilly wind and mists would afflict his jade-like body. When his ministers and others submitted to the throne that a new palace should be built, the emperor said, "It is the farming season, the people would surely be distressed. We should wait until fall to build it. To be afflicted by the dampness means that one is not accepted by the earth; to be affected by wind and rain means that one is not in harmony with heaven. If one goes against heaven and earth, he cannot maintain his body. If one does not trouble the people, he should harmonize naturally with heaven and earth." So saying that if he harmonized with heaven and earth they would not afflict his body, after all he did not build a new palace, but abode in the old building.

Even a worldling thus thought more of the people than of his own body. How much more so should children of Buddha, inheriting the custom of the house of the Tathagata, take compassion on all living beings, as upon an only child.

One should not revile and torment his attendants or followers on the excuse that they are his servants. How much more so should fellow students and equal companions respect and honor the abiding Ancients of venerable years, just as if they were the Tathagata: the words of the precepts are clear about this.

Therefore students of the present time as well should think of doing what would be good for others, without distinguishing in your hearts between high and low, relative or stranger, even though this does not show outwardly and is unknown to others. Whether in respect to matters great or small, no one should torment or break the hearts of other people.

When the Tathagata was in the world, many outsiders slandered and scorned the Tathagata. The Buddha's disciples asked, "The Tathagata has always taken gentleness as fundamental, and has compassion in his heart; all living beings should honor him equally. Why do such stubborn creatures as these exist?"

The Buddha said, "When I led a congregation in the past, I often reprimanded my disciples with acts of scolding and carping. Because of this, the present situation is as it is." So it is to be seen among the books of monastic rules.[1]

Thus, even if one leads a group, acting as the chief Elder in residence, when he is going to correct the errors of his disciples, he should not make use of scolding or criticizing speech. If he just uses gentle words to admonish and encourage, then those who would obey will still obey.

Even more should students completely give up using coarse language to family and dependents, or vilely slandering others. Be very careful.

7

HE ALSO SAID,

The concern of a patchrobed monk should be to maintain the comportment of Buddhas and Patriarchs. Most importantly, above all one should not covet property and wealth. The reason for that is that the profundity of the Tathagata's compassion is difficult to fathom, even by way of simile. But all that he did was for the sake of living beings. He would not do even the slightest thing that would not be of benefit to living beings.

That is because as long as he was the crown prince of a universal monarch, whereas once he had succeeded to the throne he could have done with the world as he liked, taking pity on his disciples with treasures, and swaddled them with his possessions, why did he abandon his title, and practice begging on his own? Because there must certainly have been some useful conditioning factors both for the sake of beings of the final age, and to help his disciples traverse the Way, he did not keep his property and wealth, but practiced begging for food. Thenceforth, those of the patriarchal teachers of India and China who were also known by others as good people, were all at the extremity of poverty and begged for their food.

All the more do the Patriarchs of our sect only exhort that we should not accumulate property and wealth. Even in the Scholastic sects, when they praise this [Zen] sect, above all they praise poverty: in the books and records that have come down to us as well, this poverty is recorded and praised. I have never heard of anyone rich in material wealth who carried out the Way of the Buddhas. All those known as good Buddhists wore patched rags and always begged for food.

In the beginning, when the Zen sect was first called a worthy foundation and its meditating monks were considered different from others, it was because even in the old days when they were abiding amongst others in the Teaching Halls and Discipline Cloisters[1] and the like, they forsook their bodies and were poor people. In the inherited tradition of this fundamental sect, this fact before all should be known. You do not need to depend on the reasoning of the words of the Sage's Teaching: there was even a time when I myself owned fields, gardens, and the rest; and there was a time too when I possessed property and wealth. As I compare the state of my body and mind of that time to now, when I am so poor that I hardly have a robe and bowl, I feel that my state of mind right now is better. This is evident proof.

8

He also said,

An Ancient said, "If you are not as good as that person, do not talk about how he acts."

What this intends to say is that if you have not studied and do not know the merits of the person, when you see the person make a mistake, you should not think, "That's a good person, but the deed is bad; so good people also do bad things, don't they!" Just take the person's virtues, do not grasp the person's faults. The saying that the gentleman holds to virtue but does not hold to fault, means the same thing.

9

One day he said,

People should cultivate secret virtue. If they cultivate hidden virtues, there will surely be unseen bestowal of manifest benefits.

Even if they are mud or wooden images, coarse and crude, you should respect images of Buddhas; even though they be shabby productions of yellow scrolls and red rolls, you should believe and honor the scriptures; even if they are undisciplined, shameless monks, you should look up to and accept the essence of monkhood. If you pay honor and respect within your heart, with a believing mind, you will certainly experience evident blessing. Just because they are undisciplined, shameless monks, roughly depicted Buddhas, or shabby copies of the scriptures, if you therefore do not believe in or respect them, you will certainly experience punishment. Being the proper legacy of the Tathagata, they are Buddhist images, scriptures, and monks, who are a blessing to humans and gods. Therefore, if you take refuge in them and honor them, there will surely be benefit. If you do not believe, you will incur punishment. No matter how exceptionally debased they may be, we should take refuge in and honor the realms of the Three Treasures.

To indulge in evil doings with the excuse that "A Zen monk does not cultivate good, nor does he have any use for virtue," is extremely one-sided. I have never heard of any precedent for indulgence in evil in the ancient standards. The Zen Master T'an Hsia T'ien Jan[1] burned a wooden Buddha; though it is exactly something like this which seems to be evil doing, it was a device to explain the Teaching at a certain level.

When we look at the record of that master's deeds, when he sat it was always with dignity, when he stood it was always with proper bearing; he was always as though facing an honored guest. Even when sitting down for a little while he always crossed his legs and folded his hands; he took care of the community property as one would take care of his eyes. Whenever there were any diligent in practice, he would not fail to praise them; even a little bit of good he deemed important. His ordinary mode of action was exceptionally excellent; his record is set down as a mirror and guide for the monasteries.

Moreover, from what we learn of all the masters who have attained the Way, of the former Patriarchs who were awakened to the Path, they all maintained disciplined behavior, regulated their conduct, and considered even a little bit of goodness to be important. I have never heard of any masters who were awakened to the Path who made little of good roots.

Therefore, students, if you wish to follow the Way of the Patriarchs, do not take good roots lightly. You should be wholehearted in faith and aspiration. The Buddhas' and Patriarchs' journey on the Path is always where manifold good accumulates. Once you have perceived that all dharmas are the Buddha Dharma, then you should know that evil is definitely evil and is far from the Way of Buddhas and Patriarchs, and that good is definitely good and becomes an affinity with the Buddhist Way. If so, how could you not esteem the realms of the Three Treasures?

10

HE ALSO SAID,

Now if you want to travel the Way of Buddhas and Patriarchs, then expect nothing, seek nothing, grasp nothing; without thought of profit you should go the Way of the former sages, and practice the behavior of the successive Patriarchs.

If you say that having cut off all seeking, one should not seek the fruit of enlightenment, and therefore you give up practice and remain in your former evil ways, after all, you have stuck to your original desires and fallen back into your old pit.

If you do not harbor any expectations at all, but just to be a bit of blessing to humanity and the gods, maintain the proper dignity of monkhood, consider what actions would help rescue living beings, joyfully cultivate all virtues, abandoning your former evil, yet without lingering over your present good, if you continue to pass your whole lifetime like this, the Ancients would call you one who has "broken through the black lacquer bucket."[1] Such is the conduct of Buddhas and Patriarchs.

11

ONE DAY A MONK CAME AND ASKED about how to concentrate on the study of the Way. Accordingly, the master taught him,

"A person who studies the Way first of all must be poor. If his possessions are many, he will surely lose his will. If householders who study the Way are still bound by their wealth, cling to their houses, and associate with their relations, even if they have an appropriate aspiration, there are many factors veiling them from the Way.

"Although from ancient times many lay people have engaged in this study, even those among them who were known to be good still did not compare to monks. While monks have no possessions except three robes and one bowl, do not think about where to live, and are not greedy for food or clothing, if they study the Path unbendingly, each will obtain benefit according to his capacity. The reason for this is that poverty is near to the Way.

"Mr. P'ang,[1] although a layman, was not inferior to a monk: his name is remembered in the Zen centers because when the man began to engage in meditation, he took all his family wealth and went to throw it in the sea. People remonstrated with him, saying,

'You should either give it to someone else, or use it for Buddhist services.'

"Then he answered them, 'Since I considered it an enemy, I have abandoned it; knowing it to be harmful, how could I give it to others? Wealth is an enemy which causes trouble to body and mind.' So after all he threw it all in the sea.

"Afterwards, he wove bamboo baskets and sold them to make a living. Though he was a layman, it was when he had thus abandoned his property and wealth that he was known as a good man. So much the more must monks abandon it altogether."

12

A MONK SAID, "In the monasteries of China, there is established communal property, and such things as are in the permanent endowment; thus they serve as sustaining factors for the monks in their practice of the Way, and they have no such worries. Since there is no such establishment in our country, if [supplies] are totally given up, it would become quite a disturbance to the practice of the Way. Therefore I feel that some consideration should be made for food and clothing for sustenance; what about it?"

Dogen said, "Not so. Rather than China, it happens more in this country that people support monks without reason, and give people things they don't deserve. I don't know about others, but I have practiced this thing and realized its truth. I have already passed ten years without possessing anything at all, and without making any plans. To think of storing up even a little bit of wealth is a great problem. Even if you do not think of how to accumulate it, it is there naturally. Everyone has his lot in life; heaven and earth bestow it. Even though one does not himself run seeking for it, one will surely have it.

"How much the more so for Buddhists, who have the endowment left by the Tathagata; without seeking it is naturally obtained: if you just abandon everything and practice the Way, you will have it by nature. This is the evident proof."

13

HE ALSO SAID,

People who study the Way often say, "If we do such a thing, the people of the world may criticize us." This is very wrong.

No matter how people may criticize you, as long as it is the conduct of Buddhas and Patriarchs, or according to the principles of the Sage's Teaching, you should follow and practice it. And even if everyone in the world praises it, if it is an act which is not in the principles of the Sage's Teaching, or is something that the Patriarchs would not do, you should not carry it out.

For this reason, if the people of the world, be they relatives or strangers, should praise you or revile you, even if because of that you go along with their ideas, when your own life is ending and you are drawn by evil actions to the brink of falling into evil ways, those people cannot save you in any way. And even if you are slandered and despised by everyone, if you follow and practice the Way of the Buddhas and Patriarchs, because it can really and truly help you, you should not fail to practice the Way with the excuse that others will criticize you.

Furthermore, those people who criticize or who praise in this way are not necessarily those who have mastered and proved the practices of Buddhas and Patriarchs. How could it be possible to judge the Way of Buddhas and Patriarchs on the basis of worldly good and evil?

Therefore we should not go along with the sentiments of worldly people; simply because it is the fact that we should follow and practice the Buddha's Way, we should practice it wholeheartedly.

14

ALSO A CERTAIN MONK SAID, "My aged mother is still alive, and I am her only son. It is solely due to my support that she gets along in the world. My gratitude and love are profound, and my desire to be filial and obedient is deep. Because of this I go along somewhat with society and go along with people, using the power of their benevolence to supply my mother with food and clothes. If I were to forsake society and dwell in seclusion, my mother could hardly hope to live for even one day. Yet it is also a difficult thing to remain in the world because of this, and thus not enter completely into the Way of Buddhas. If there is a reason why I should, after all, give up and so be able to enter the Path, what is the gist of it?''

Dogen replied, ''This is a difficult matter; it is not for anyone else to decide. You must just think it over thoroughly on your own, and if you sincerely have a will to enter the Way of Buddhas, then if you settle whatever preparations or expedients are necessary to provide for the secure livelihood of your mother, and enter the Buddhist Path, it will be good on both sides.

''Anything that is earnestly desired is attained: though it be a powerful opponent, a voluptuous woman, or a precious jewel, if one's earnest desire is deep enough, there must surely be some kind of means which will develop. This even has the unseen help of the benevolent spirits of sky and earth, and will not fail to work out.

''We read that the Sixth Patriarch of Ts'ao Ch'i[1] was a wood-cutter in Hsin province who sold firewood to support his mother. One day in the market place he heard a traveler reciting the Diamond Scripture and awakened his mind; when he left his mother to seek out Huang Mei, he obtained ten ounces of silver to supply food and clothing for his mother. In this case too, it seems as if heaven might have given it to him because he was earnest in his desire.

''You should consider this carefully; it is most reasonable. If you wait out your mother's life, and then afterwards enter unimpeded into the Buddhist Way, successively fulfilling your original aspirations, it would be wonderful. Yet you never know: neither old nor young are safe, so supposing your mother lingered on for a long time while you yourself die first; since your preparations would have gone wrong, you will regret not having entered the Buddhist Path, and your old mother will be submerged in guilt for not having permitted you to do so: then there would be no benefit for either one, and you will incur mutual reproach; how will it be then? Once you have given up your life to enter the Way of Buddhas, even if your old mother should starve to death, would not the virtue of having allowed her only son to enter the Way be a good help to her attainment of the Way?

"Although it is, of course, gratitude and love which are difficult to abandon even over vast aeons and many lives, if you forsake them now that you have got a human body in this life and have encountered the Teaching of Buddha, this is the essence of true requital of debt. How could this not be in conformity with the will of Buddha? I have read that if one child leaves home, seven generations of ancestors obtain release.[2] There is also the reason that why should you think only of one generation of evanescent life, thus missing the opportunity for eternal peace and happiness? You must judge these carefully on your own."

NOTE TO 1

1. See note 4 to book I, section 13.

NOTES TO 5

1. "Senior" is literally "the head seat"; the order of precedence in a monks' hall is determined by seniority in number of years ordained. A number of the head seats, however, are occupied by monks chosen especially to fulfill certain functions in the organization of the community.
2. The monks' hall is divided into front and rear when the congregation is large. The monk occupying the head seat of the rear hall is supposed to be a model for the community, and fulfills the duties of the head seat of the front hall when the latter is lacking.
3. The head seat of the front hall leads the community in meditation and disciplines the monks, sometimes lecturing or giving private instruction in place of the teaching master. This position is to be filled by someone qualified to be even a Great Elder, or teaching master of a temple. As deputies of the master, the positions of head seat of the front and rear are both very important offices.

NOTE TO 6

1. *Vinaya*; the evolution or incident of each monastic rule is provided as context to the precepts; these are among the oldest books of the Buddhist canon, different from the so-called Bodhisattva Precepts mentioned in book I.

NOTE TO 7

1. Temples devoted to lecture and study of scriptures, or to the observance of the ancient modes of monastic conduct, as given in the *Vinaya*. The independent Zen monastery is usually said to have been founded by Pai Chang Huai Hai (720–814). See book I, section 2.

NOTE TO 9

1. T'ien Jan (739–824), whose name means "natural" or "spontaneous," was a successor to the great Shih T'ou Hsi Ch'ien. Once, at Hui Lin temple during the wintertime, he burnt a wooden image of Buddha to warm himself. Someone

scolded him for this act, but he said he was doing it to get the *sharira,* relics of a Buddha's cremation. When the man said that there are no relics in a mere piece of wood, T'ien Jan said, "Then what are you blaming me for?"

NOTE TO 10

1. A lacquer bucket is a metaphor for ignorance.

NOTE TO 11

1. P'ang Yun was a friend of T'ien Jan (see section 9), and was first awakened by Shih T'ou Hsi Ch'ien; later he was completely enlightened under the tutelage of Ma Tsu Tao I (see book II, section 22), and is known as the latter's successor. He was originally a man of the landlord class, and a scholar of Confucianism. Later, his wife, son, daughter, and himself were all known as enlightened people. After breaking up his household and throwing away his possessions, he traveled around with his daughter, weaving bamboo goods for a living, and visiting the leading Zen masters of the day (most of whom were successors of Shih T'ou and Ma Tsu). Many of his sayings, conversations with Zen masters, and about three hundred of his poems, have been recorded and left to posterity.

NOTES TO 14

1. Hui Neng (638–713), the Sixth Patriarch of Zen in China, and one of the most illustrious figures of the sect. His father had been an official and was exiled to the far south of the Chinese empire (Canton); he died when the Patriarch was still a boy, leaving him to support his mother by cutting wood. The Diamond Scripture (*Prajnaparamita Vajracchedika Sutra*) was one of the scriptures used by the Fifth Patriarch Hung Jen in his teaching (on Mt. Huang Mei); when, according to tradition, Hui Neng heard the sentence, "Without any place of abode should one arouse the mind," he was suddenly awakened and determined to seek out the Fifth Patriarch.

2. This idea was apparently invented to reconcile the Buddhist Way of leaving home to the secular Chinese Confucian tradition, which demands that a man have children to maintain the sacrifices at the ancestral shrine.

BOOK IV

1

ONE DAY AFTER INDIVIDUAL STUDY meetings, he said,

Students of the Way, do not cling to your own understanding. Even if there is something you do understand, you should ask yourself whether there might still be something not fully resolved, or whether there may be some meaning which is better than this; seek far and wide for those who know, and inquire also into the words of people of former times.

Yet do not cling fast even to the words of those people of old. Thinking that this too may be wrong, even though you believe it, if there should be something superior to this next, then you should turn to that.

2

HE ALSO SAID,

The National Teacher Hui Chung of Nan Yang[1] asked the purple-vested imperial attendant monk Lin,[2] "Where do you come from?"

The attendant replied, "From south of the city."

The Teacher said, "What color is the grass south of the city?"

The attendant replied, "It is yellow."

The Teacher then asked a page boy, "What color is the grass south of the city?"

The boy said, "It is yellow."

The Teacher said, "Even this boy can also be granted purple vestments and discuss the mysterious in the imperial presence."

70

Thus he was saying that even a page boy, as the teacher of a nation's emperor, could reply with the true color; your view does not surpass the ordinary way. Later, someone said, "Where is the fault of the imperial attendant monk failing to transcend the ordinary? The page boy too spoke of the real color. This is the very making of a real teacher." So he did not accept the National Teacher's interpretation. Thus we know that one need not necessarily depend upon the words of the Ancients, but must only think of what is really true. Although a doubting mind is bad, still it is wrong to cling to that which you should not believe, or to fail to ask about a meaning which you should seek.

3

HE ALSO INSTRUCTED,

The foremost concern of a student is first to detach from the notion of self. To detach from the notion of self means that we must not cling to this body. Even if you have thoroughly studied the stories of the Ancients, and sit constantly like iron or stone, if you are attached to your body and do not detach from it, you could not find the Way of Buddhas and Patriarchs even in ten thousand aeons, in a thousand lifetimes.

All the more, though you may say you have understood the temporary and true methods of teaching, and the true Exoteric and Esoteric doctrines, if you do not leave off your feeling of attachment to your body, you are idly counting the treasures of others, without having a half-penny of your own.

I only ask that students sit quietly and look into the beginning and end of this body as it truly is. The body, limbs, hair, and skin come from the two drops of father's semen and mother's blood; when the breath ceases, they separate and decay in the mountains and fields, eventually turning into mud and earth. What do you have to cling to as your body?

How much more is this so when we look at it from the point of view of the elements; in the accumulation and dispersal of the eighteen realms,[1] which elements can you definitely consider as your

own body? Whether it is within the Teachings or outside of the
Teachings,[2] the fact is the same, that neither beginning nor end of
one's body can be grasped is the essential point to be aware of in
practicing the Way. If you have first arrived at this truth, the Real
Buddha-Way is something that is obviously so.

4

ONE DAY HE INSTRUCTED,

An Ancient said, "Familiarity with good people is like walking
through mist and dew; although they do not drench your garment,
in time it becomes imbued with moisture."[1] What this means to say
is that if one becomes well acquainted with the good, without realizing it, he himself becomes a good man. In the case of the servant boy
who attended the master Chu T'i,[2] although it is not known when he
studied and we do not read when it was that he practiced, because he
was in the company of someone who had studied for a long time, he
realized the Way.

In sitting meditation as well, if you do it for a long time, you will
spontaneously become suddenly aware of the Great Matter, and
should know that sitting meditation is the correct entrance.

5

ON JANUARY 28, 1236, Dogen first requested me, Ejo, to occupy the
first seat[1] of Kosho Temple. Thus after an informal meeting, he first
asked me as head monk to take up the whisk and preach.[2] I was the
first head monk of Kosho Temple.

The message of the informal meeting was to bring out the matter
of the transmission of the Buddhist Teaching, according to the
method of our sect. [Dogen said,]

"The first Patriarch came from the West and dwelt in Shao Lin,
awaiting a man of potential. As he bided his time, sitting facing a
wall, in a certain year, during the coldest part of winter, Shen
Kuang[3] came seeking him. The First Patriarch knew that he was a

vessel of the Supreme Vehicle, so he received him: the robe and the Teaching were handed down together,[4] their descendants spread throughout the land, and the True Teaching is now widely known.

"Now this temple invites its first head monk, and today, for the first time, let the 'taking up of the whisk' be carried out. Do not worry how small the congregation is; do not be concerned that you are a beginner. At Fen Yang[5] there were only seven or eight people, and at Yao Shan[6] there were no more than ten. Nevertheless, they each carried out the Way of Buddhas and Patriarchs. This was called the flourishing of the monasteries.

"Have you not read about awakening to the Way through the sound of bamboo, of enlightening the mind by the sight of peach blossoms?[7] Do you think there is any cleverness or stupidity in the bamboo? Any delusion or enlightenment? How could there be shallow or profound, wise or stupid among the flowers? Although the flowers bloom every year, that doesn't mean that everyone attains the Way. Although the bamboo echoes from time to time, that does not mean that all who hear it witness the Path. It is only by virtue of long study and persevering practice, with the supporting help of hard effort in discernment of the Way, that they realized the Path and understood the mind. It is not that the sound of the bamboo alone was sharp, nor is it that the color of the flowers was especially lush. Although the echo of bamboo is marvelous, it does not sound of itself; it depends upon the help of a piece of tile to make a sound. Although the color of the flowers is beautiful, they do not bloom of themselves; they need the spring breeze to open.

"The conditions for the study of the Way are also like this; although the Way is complete in everyone, the realization of the Way depends upon collective conditions. Although individuals may be clever, the practice of the Way is done by means of collective power. Therefore, now you should make your minds as one, set your aspirations in one direction, and study thoroughly, seek and inquire.

"Jade becomes a vessel by carving and polishing. A man becomes humane by cultivation and polish. What gem has highlights to begin with? What person is clever from the outset? You must carve and polish, train and cultivate them. Humble yourselves and do not relax your study of the Way.

"An Ancient said, 'Do not pass time in vain.'[8] Now I ask you, does time stop because you value it? Does it not stop even though you value it? You must realize that time does not pass by in vain; it is man who passes it in vain. This means that people, like time, should not go idly by, but should earnestly study the Way.

"Thus participation in the study must be done with like minds. It is not that I am taking it easy from teaching by myself alone: the way in which the Buddhas and Patriarchs carried out the Way was generally always like this. Although there were many who realized the Way by following the instructions of the Tathagata, there were also those who realized the Way because of Ananda.[9] Do not belittle the new head monk, saying that he is not a man of capacity. Recite the story of Tung Shan's 'three pounds of hemp'[10] to instruct your fellows.''

So he got down from the seat, and after causing the drum to be sounded again, the head monk took the whisk. This was the first "taking of the whisk" at Kosho Temple. Ejo was thirty-nine years old.

6

ONE DAY HE INSTRUCTED,

Ordinary people say, "Who does not desire fine clothing? Who is not fond of rich flavors?" Nevertheless, people who wish to know the Way enter into the mountains, sleep in the clouds, endure cold, and endure hunger. It is not that our predecessors experienced no suffering; it is that they endured it to preserve the Way. Thus, people of later times heard of this, aspired to their way, and respected their virtue.

Even in the ordinary world, those who are wise are like this; should the Way of Buddhas not also be so? Even the Ancients did not all have [Buddha's] golden bones; even when he was in the world, not all of them were of superior capacity. In considering the various monks in the context of the collection of behavioral codes [the *Vinaya-pitaka*], there were those who developed unbelievably far out states of mind. Nevertheless, we read that later on they all attained the Way and became Arhats.[1] Thus, even though we too may be mean and inept, knowing that if we rouse our minds to practice, we shall surely attain the Way; then our minds are aroused.

In the past, too, they all endured pain and forbore cold and cultivated their practice in the midst of their distress. Students now, even though you be in sore distress, still you should just force yourselves to study the Way.

7

HE INSTRUCTED,

Students of the Way, the fact that you fail to attain enlightenment is just because you retain your former views. Although you do not even know who originally taught you, yet you think that what is called "mind" is thought and knowledge; when I say that the mind is plants and trees, you do not believe it. When I speak of Buddha, you think that it must have auspicious features and a radiant halo; when I explain that Buddha is tiles and pebbles, it startles your ears.[1] Such grasping views are not transmitted by your fathers, nor did your mothers teach them. It is just that you have tacitly come to believe them for no reason over a long period of time, by picking up what people say. Therefore, because it is the established Teaching of Buddhas and Patriarchs, if it says that mind is plants and trees, know plants and trees to be mind; and if it says that Buddha is tiles and pebbles, believe that tiles and pebbles themselves are Buddha: if you go on changing your original convictions, you should find the Way.

An Ancient said, "Although sun and moon are bright, the floating clouds cover them; though the tangled orchid vines are about to bloom, the autumn wind withers them." The *Cheng Kuan Cheng Yao* ["Essentials of Government, compiled in the Cheng Kuan Era"] quotes this as a simile for a wise king with evil ministers. Now I say, "Though the floating clouds cover, it won't be for long; though the autumn wind withers them, they will bloom again." Even if his ministers are evil, if the wisdom of the king is unbending, it should not be influenced by them. Now if you would know the Way of Buddhas, you must also be like this. No matter how bad a state of mind you get into, if you keep strong and hold out over a long period of time, in truth the floating clouds must vanish and the autumn wind must cease.

8

ONE DAY HE INSTRUCTED,

When students are beginners, whether they have the mind of the Way or not, they should carefully read and study the Sagely Teachings of the sutras and shastras.[1]

I first aroused the aspiration for enlightenment somewhat because of impermanence; eventually I left the Tendai school, and as I sought all over, cultivating the Way, during the interval when I was staying at Kennin Temple, because I did not meet a true teacher and there were no worthy companions, I went astray and gave rise to wrong ideas.

Because even the teachers of the Way taught first to become equally as good as the past scholars, to be known to the nation and famous throughout the land, even as I studied the doctrines of the Teaching, I thought first of being equal to the ancient wise men of Japan, and wanted to be the same even as the Great Teachers.[2] As I read such books as the *Biographies of Eminent Monks*[3] and the *Continued Biographies of Eminent Monks,* and saw how it was with the eminent monks and Buddhists of China, they were not like my present teachers. And since I realized that a state of mind such as I had developed is held in contempt in all the sutras, shastras, biographies and such, when I came to think about what is right, even if one wants name and fame, rather than be well thought of by the inferior people of the present time, one should only have shame before the sages of antiquity and the good people of later ages. And even if one thinks of equaling someone, rather than the people of Japan, we should be ashamed before the past masters and eminent monks of China and India, and think of being equal to such as them. We should even want to equal the hidden beings of the heavens, to Buddhas and Bodhisattvas.

After I had grasped this truth, I considered the Great Teachers and others of Japan as like dirt or tiles, and my former state of body and mind was completely changed. When we look at the actions of the Buddha during his lifetime, we see that he forsook the rank of king, and entered into the mountains and forests; even after he had realized the Way, he begged for food all his life. In the *Vinaya* it says, "Knowing his house was not a home, he abandoned his house and left home."

An Ancient said, "Do not be so proud as to hope to equal the great wise ones; do not be so mean as to hope to equal the ignoble." What this means is that both are conceits. Even if you are in a high place, do not forget that you may fall. Even if you are safe, do not forget danger. Even though you are alive today, do not think that you will also be so tomorrow. The imminent danger of death is right at our feet.

9

He pointed out,

Foolish people think and say pointless things. There is an aged nun working here, who while showing shame at her present low position, still tells people about how she was once high class. Even if people now believe it was so, I don't see what the use of it is; I think it is quite useless.

It seems as though this feeling is present in everyone's thoughts. And it is obvious how they lack the mind of the Way. One should change such feelings and be a little like other people.

Also there is a certain lay monk who is extremely lacking in the mind of the Way. Because he is nevertheless a friend, I want to tell him to pray to the Buddhas and spirits that his mind for the Way be aroused, but he would certainly become angry and our relationship would be strained. However, as long as his mind for the Way is not aroused, complacence can be of no use to either of us.

10

He instructed,

Of old it was said, "Reflect thrice before speaking." What this means is that whenever you are going to say something, or whenever you are going to do something, only after reflecting three times should you speak or act. The intention of that ancient Confucian was that upon considering three times, if each time it is good, then you should say or do it. The meaning of the wise ones of China when they spoke of reflecting thrice was that one should reflect many times; that one should think before speaking, think before acting, and if each time you consider something, it is always good, then do or say it.

Patchrobed monks also must be like this. Because there might be something wrong in what you think or say, first reflect upon whether or not it is in conformity with the Way of Buddhas, carefully consider whether or not there will be any benefit for self and others, and only then, if it should be good, you should so act and speak. If a wayfarer always watches over his heart in this way, he would not go against the will of Buddha his whole life long.

In the past, when I first entered Kennin Temple, the community of monks guarded their actions of body, mouth, and mind as well as they could, each determined not to say or do anything which would be detrimental to the Buddhist Way or to the interests of other people. As long as the remains of the high priest Eisai's virtue lingered there, it was like this. These days, though, there is no such propriety.

Students now should know that if there is something which definitely would have worth for self and others and for the sake of the Buddhist Way, you should even forget about your own bodies to say or do it. As for those things which are pointless, do not do or say them. When venerable Elders are speaking or acting, juniors should not interrupt. This was a regulation of the Buddha; consider it carefully.

This mind which forgets the body to consider the Way exists even among secular people. In olden times there was a man of the state of Chao[1] named Lin Hsiang-ju; although he was a lower class man, because he was intelligent, he was employed by the king of Chao and handled the affairs of the land.

Once, as the envoy of the king of Chao, he was sent to carry a gem known as the Jewel of Chao into the state of Ch'in.[2] Because the king of Ch'in had said he would give fifteen cities in exchange for that jewel, the king of Chao sent Hsiang-ju to carry it; at this point, the other ministers conferred with each other, saying, "To entrust such a jewel to the hands of such a lowly man as Hsiang-ju makes it seem as if there were no people in our land. It would be a disgrace to us other ministers; we would be scorned by future generations."

At the time, someone secretly informed Hsiang-ju that they were plotting to kill him on the way and steal the jewel, and told him that he should decline this mission in order to save his life. Thereupon Hsiang-ju said, "I dare not decline. When I take the jewel to Ch'in as the envoy of the king, it would be a joy for me that later generations would hear Hsiang-ju was killed by treacherous ministers. Although my body will die, my reputation as a worthy man should remain." So saying, he went after all. When the other ministers heard of his words, they said that they could not kill such a man, so they gave up the idea.

Although Hsiang-ju eventually saw the king of Ch'in and presented the jewel to him, it seemed that the king of Ch'in did not want to give the fifteen cities in return. Thus, Hsiang-ju, devising a plan, said to the king of Ch'in, "There is a flaw in that jewel; I will show you." So he asked for the jewel back, and then said, "As I look upon the king's face, it appears that you want to keep your fifteen cities; therefore I will use my head to break this jewel against that bronze pillar." As he looked at the king with angry eyes and moved towards the pillar, he looked as though he would really break the jewel.

Then the king of Ch'in said, "Don't break the jewel. I will give the fifteen cities. You keep the jewel while the arrangements are being made." But Hsiang-ju secretly had someone take the jewel back to his own land.

Later, when the kings of Chao and Ch'in were amusing themselves at a place called Min Ch'ih, the king of Ch'in told the king of Chao to play the lute, at which he was expert. The king of Chao picked the lute without even consulting Hsiang-ju. At the time Hsiang-ju was angry that the king of Chao had obeyed the order of the king of Ch'in, and went himself to make the king of Ch'in play a flute. He said to the king of Ch'in, "You are skillful on the flute, and the king of Chao wants to hear you, so you should play." When he said this, the king of Ch'in refused. Hsiang-ju said, "If you refuse, I'll kill you."

At that point, a Ch'in general approached with his sword. Hsiang-ju glared at him with his eyes bulging out. The general was frightened and retreated without drawing his sword; so after all, the king of Ch'in said he would play the flute.

Later, when Hsiang-ju became a top minister and handled the affairs of the land, another chief minister was jealous of the fact that he himself was not so entrusted with the responsibility, and so he tried to kill Hsiang-ju. At that time Hsiang-ju fled and hid here and there; he did not even appear at the court when it was in session—he appeared to be afraid.

Then Hsiang-ju's retainers said, "It would be an easy matter to kill that other minister; why do you hide in fear?"

Hsiang-ju said, "It is not that I fear him. I stood off a general of Ch'in with my eyes and even stole the jewel of Ch'in; needless to say, I could kill that minister. However, the raising of an army and the stockpiling of weapons is for the purpose of defending against an enemy nation. Now as great right- and left-hand ministers who protect our country, if the two of us are at odds, and we start a war in which one of us dies, then one side will be weakened. Thus the neighboring countries will rejoice and will mobilize their armies for war. For this reason, since I wish for both parties to remain unharmed to protect our nation, I will not start a fight with him."

When the other minister heard of this speech, he was ashamed and returned to pay obeisance. The two men then worked together to govern the country.

It was thus that Hsiang-ju forgot his own body and was mindful of the Way. Now in thinking of the Way of Buddhas as well, one's mind must be like that of Hsiang-ju. It is said that it is better to have the Way and to die than to live without the Way.

11

HE INSTRUCTED,

It is hard to determine what is good or bad. Worldly people say that it is good to wear silk, brocade, and embroidery, and they say that garments of coarse cloth and rags are bad. In the Buddhist Teaching these latter are considered good and pure, whereas gold, silver, brocade, and silk are considered bad and defiled. Thus it is in respect to all things.

In my case too, when I make a little rhyme and write some fancy words, it even happens that some lay people say it is exceptional. Then again, there are also people who criticize me for being able to do such things, inasmuch as I am a leaver of home and a student of the Way. Which is to be definitely taken as good, and which is to be abandoned as bad?

It is written [in the *Vinaya*], "What is praised as pure in character is called good; what is scorned as impure in character is called bad." It is also said, "That which would incur pain is called bad; that which should bring about happiness is called good."

In this way should one carefully discriminate; seeing real good, one should practice it, and seeing real evil, one should shun it. Because a monk is something that comes from within purity, he considers as good and pure that which would not arouse human desires.

12

HE INSTRUCTED,

Many people of the world say, "Although one may have the aspiration to study the Way, the world is in its Last Age, and people are inferior, unfit to carry out practice according to the Way. One should just go the easy way according to his capacity, and think of forming a basis whereupon one might hope for awakening in another lifetime."[1]

Now I say that these words are completely wrong. In the Buddhist Teaching, the setting of the three periods of True, Semblance, and Final is a kind of temporary expedient. When the Buddha was in the world, the mendicants were not necessarily all outstanding; there were also those who were unbelievably debased, with inferior faculties. Therefore, the Buddha's establishment of various kinds of disciplinary rules was all for the sake of evil beings, people of inferior faculties.

Everyone is a vessel of the Buddhist Teaching: do not think you are not fit for it. If you follow and practice it, you should obtain realization. Since you have minds, you should be able to discriminate good from bad; you have hands and feet, so there is no reason why you can't join your palms or walk.[2] Thus the practice of the Buddhist Teaching is not a matter of choosing the vessel; each human life is a vessel of this endowment. The other realms of life, such as animals, are not suitable. People who are studying the Way should not wait for tomorrow; on this day, this hour alone, you should go in accord with the Way of the Buddhas.

13

HE INSTRUCTED,

There is a proverb which says, "The downfall of a castle comes from the whispering of words within its walls." It is also said, "When there are two opinions within a house, it cannot even buy a pin; when there is no divergence of opinion within the house, it has the means to buy even gold."

Even in the secular world, to maintain a household or safeguard a castle, without union of minds, eventually it will be ruined. How much more so should leavers of home studying under a single master harmonize like the merging of water and milk. There is also the law of sixfold harmony and respect.[1] Do not each set up separate rooms and concentrate on the study of the Way with your bodies apart, according to your individual frames of mind. It is like riding on one boat to cross the sea; you should study the Path in the same way, with unity of mind, uniformity of behavior, mutually reforming each other's faults, and following each other's good points. This is the form that has been practiced since the time the Buddha was in the world.

14

HE INSTRUCTED,

At the time that the meditation master Fang Hui of Mt. Yang Ch'i[1] first took up teaching, since his temple was old and dilapidated and it was a hardship to the monks, the director of affairs told him it should be repaired.

Fang Hui said, "Though the building is broken down, still it must be better than open ground under the trees. If one spot is leaking, then you should go sit in a spot where it doesn't leak in order to meditate. If the community would attain enlightenment by the building of a hall, then it should be built even with gold and jewels. Enlightenment does not depend on how good or bad one's dwelling place may be; it should only be a matter of how great or small the accomplishment in sitting meditation."

The next day, in a community lecture, he said,

> While Yang Ch'i's abode has chinks in the walls,
> The whole sitting platform is covered with pearls of snow.
> Drawing in their necks, they sigh in the dark.

After a long pause, he said, "I think back to the Ancients sitting under the trees."

It is not only the Way of Buddhahood; the way of government is also like this. Emperor T'ai Tsung of T'ang did not build a palace.

Lung Ya said, "To learn the Way, first one must, for a time, learn about poverty. Having learned about poverty, only after becoming poor, is the Way then near."

From of old in the time of Shakyamuni up until the present day, I have never seen or heard of a true and genuine student of the Way who possessed abundant wealth.

15

ONE DAY A VISITING MONK SAID, "In recent times, the way of fleeing society is that each individual makes provisions for his own food and other needs, preparing so that he will have no worry about them later. Though these are minor concerns, still they are sustaining factors in the study of the Way. If they are lacking, one's efforts will be thwarted. Now according to what I have heard of how it is with you, you make no such provisions at all, but merely leave it to fate. If this is true, won't you have some trouble later on?"

Dogen replied, "Everything has its precedents: it is not that I presume to abide by my private prejudices. All the Buddhas and Patriarchs of India and China were like this. If one pursued selfish schemes to stay alive, there would be no end to it.[1] Also, it is impossible to plan for sure for the concern of the morrow. This way is that which has been practiced by all the Buddhas and Patriarchs and there is nothing selfish about it. If something is lacking or we have no food at all, then when the time comes I will devise some expedient. It is not something to think any further about."

16

HE INSTRUCTED,

There is a story, though I don't know if it is true or not, about the late lay monk, Councillor Jimyoin;[1] one time when a highly treasured sword belonging to him was stolen, since the thief was among his own warrior band, the other warriors found him out and brought him to the lay monk, who said, "This is not my sword; this is an injustice." So saying, he handed back the sword.

Though it was certainly his sword, everyone knew that he had given it back out of consideration for the shame and disgrace of that warrior; in spite of everything, that time he let it go by without incident, and therefore his descendants prospered.[2]

Even in the conventional world, people with heart are like this. How much more so should leavers of home have such a heart. Since people who leave home never have any personal property, they consider wisdom and virtue to be their treasure. In a case where another is wrong, lacking in the mind of the Way, one should not bring it out directly and put him down; one should use tact and speak in such a way as to avoid arousing his resentment.

It is said that the way of the coarse and violent does not remain long. Even if you chastise justly, if your language is rough, that justice won't last long. Petty people of inferior capacities inevitably are angered at the slightest harsh word from others, thinking of their shame and disgrace. Great people of superior character should not be like this. Magnanimous people are otherwise; even when they are attacked, they do not think of revenge. Nowadays in Japan there are many petty people. It is necessary to be careful.

NOTES TO 2

1. Hui Chung (? -775) was a successor to the Sixth Patriarch Hui Neng. He first saw the Patriarch when he was only sixteen years old; after receiving the "mind seal" he lived on Mt. Pai Ya, near Nan Yang, for over forty years. Around 760, the emperor Su Tsung (r. 756-762) heard of him and summoned him to the capital, entitling him National Teacher. He was also teacher of the Emperor Tai Tsung (r. 763-775). Hui Chung was probably the last man alive who had succeeded to the Sixth Patriarch and was greatly revered by later generations.
2. Purple is the color associated with the highest status or rank; permission to wear it was to be granted by the emperor. When a monk was given an honorific title by the emperor, he was customarily given purple vestments.

NOTES TO 3

1. These are the six senses (including mind), six realms of sense objects, and the six associated consciousnesses.
2. This refers to the verbal Teachings (the "Scholastic" or "Doctrinal" schools often mentioned in this text) and the Zen Teaching (outside of scriptures). To detach from the idea that self exists is fundamental to both.

NOTES TO 4

1. From the *Kuei Shan Ching Ts'e,* "Admonitions of Kuei Shan," written by Kuei Shan Ling You (771-854) who was a successor to Pai Chang Huai Hai, previously mentioned as the founder of the sectarian Zen monastic institution.
2. The master Chu T'i used to just raise his finger whenever anyone questioned him. When someone asked his servant boy about the master's teaching, the boy also raised his finger. When Chu T'i heard of this, he cut off the boy's finger; the boy ran out crying, but Chu T'i called to him; when the boy turned his head, Chu T'i just raised his finger, whereupon the boy was suddenly enlightened. This story is found in *Wu Men Kuan,* case III.

NOTES TO 5

1. See book III, section 5, The occupant of the first seat, the "head monk," acts as deputy, or assistant to the teacher.
2. "Taking up the whisk" means to assume the role of teacher. The whisk is traditionally used to symbolize succession to the teaching, and also refers to acting as host to Dharma dialogue.
3. Usually known as Hui K'e, the Second Patriarch, who succeeded Bodhidharma.
4. Traditionally it is said that the robe of Bodhidharma was handed down through six generations of Patriarchs, symbolizing the person-to-person transmission of the so-called "Buddha Mind Seal."
5. Fen Yang Shan Chao (957-1024) was a great master of the Lin Chi sect in China.
6. Yao Shan Wei Yen (745-828) was a successor of Shih T'ou Hsi Ch'ien, and a direct ancestor of the Ts'ao Tung sect, which Dogen later transmitted to Japan.

7. See book II, section 26, and notes.
8. This is the last line of the *Ts'an T'ung Ch'i,* the famous work of Shih T'ou.
9. Ananda was the personal attendant of the Buddha; because he memorized the sutras and recited them at the first Buddhist council after the Buddha's death, thus leaving them for posterity, Dogen's statement has a wide application.
10. Tung Shan Shou Ch'u (tenth century) was a successor of Yun Men Wen Yen (founder of the Yun Men sect of Zen): once a student asked him "What is Buddha?" Tung Shan replied, "Three pounds of hemp." This story appears in the *Wu Men Kuan,* ex. XVIII, and the *Pi Yen Lu,* ex. XII.

NOTE TO 6

1. *Arhat* means "worthy (of offering)," representing the highest stage of attainment in the so-called "Lesser Vehicle," one who has attained nirvana. The *Vinaya* cites the situations in which the regulations of conduct came into being, each in respect to some fault among the monks. Dogen cites the degeneracy of some of the monks who later reformed as proof of the efficacy of discipline and practice.

NOTE TO 7

1. A monk once asked the National Teacher Hui Chung, "What is the mind of the Buddhas of Antiquity?" Hui Chung said, "Tiles and pebbles." The monk asked, "Can inanimate objects expound the Dharma?" Hui Chung said, "They are always expounding it." This is a famous story, and Dogen quotes and discusses it several times in his classic *Shobogenzo.*

NOTES TO 8

1. Sutras are the scriptures attributed to the Buddha; shastras are discourses of the Great Teachers and Patriarchs.
2. This honorific title was applied in Japan to such people as Dengyo Daishi, the founder of the Tendai school, and Kobo Daishi, the founder of the Shingon school; these are what Dogen frequently refers to as the Exoteric and Esoteric, Scholastic or Doctrinal schools, which were then the most powerful sects in Japan.
3. Compiled in the sixth century by Hui Chiao; it covers the period from the introduction of Buddhism to China in the first century A.D. until the year 519 and is a model for two later compilations of the T'ang and Sung dynasties. It is divided into various categories, such as translators, interpretors, disciplinarians, meditators, and so forth.

NOTES TO 10

1. Chao was an ancient state in northern China, east of the state of Ch'in. The incidents recounted here took place during the so-called Warring States period, when the feudal states of the Chou dynasty set themselves up as independent kingdoms and were constantly engaged in warfare and political intrigue.
2. This incident took place in 283 B.C. The state of Ch'in was rising to dominance and in the next half-century was to unify China and proclaim the first empire.

NOTES TO 12

1. This evidently refers to the *Jodo,* or Pure Land sects, which were also emerging strongly at that time; their idea was that contemporary humanity was so debased that no one could hope to attain enlightenment in this world, so the best thing

to do would be to seek to be reborn in the Pure Land, where there are not so many obstacles to enlightenment.
2. This refers to the outward aspects of the conduct of the life of study.

NOTE TO 13

1. Harmony of the threefold action of body, mouth, and mind; same discipline, same views, and same practice.

NOTES TO 14

1. Fang Hui (992–1049) was a great Chinese master of Zen, successor in the seventh generation of the Lin Chi sect and founder of what came to be known as the Yang Ch'i branch of that sect.
2. Chu Tun of Lung Ya (838–923) was a successor of Tung Shan Liang Chieh, the founder of the Ts'ao Tung sect.

NOTE TO 15

1. This is according to the Choenji text: the *rufubon* has it, "There is no end to the endowment of the White Hair; why contrive personal schemes for livelihood?" The White Hair refers to one of the Buddha's thirty-two auspicious marks, the curl of hair on his forehead; it is said that he left an infinitesimal portion of it to provide sustenance for all his disciples. This represents the offerings which since supported the Buddhist community.

NOTES TO 16

1. Ichijo Motoei (1132–1214).
2. If he had slain the warrior, it would probably have touched off a vendetta, endangering the family and partisans of Jimyoin.

BOOK V

1

ONE DAY HE INSTRUCTED,

When acting for the sake of the Buddhist Teaching, do not begrudge it your bodily life. Even lay people give up their lives for the Way, fulfilling loyalty and maintaining integrity without thinking of their families and relatives. Such is called a loyal minister and a wise man.

In ancient times, when the Emperor Kao Tsu[1] of the Han dynasty went to war with a neighboring country, the mother of one of his retainers was living in the enemy nation. The military officials suspected that he might be of two minds, and Kao Tsu also worried that he might think of his mother and go over to the enemy territory, for if so, his army might be defeated.

At this point, his mother also thought that her son might come to her country because of her, so she admonished him, saying, "Do not relax your loyalty to your army because of me. As long as I am alive, you might be of two minds." So saying, she threw herself upon a sword and perished. Because her son had never been of two minds, it is said that his intent was strong to serve his army with loyalty and integrity.

How much the more so of the patchrobed ones, aspiring to the Way of Buddhahood; when they are of absolutely undivided mind, they should truly be in accord with the Way of Buddhas. In the Way of Buddhas there are people who are originally endowed with compassion and wisdom. And even people who lack them will attain them if they study. Just cast off both body and mind, offering them to the great ocean of the Buddhist Teaching; relying on the Buddhist Teaching, do not retain your personal prejudices.

Also in the time of Kao Tsu of Han, a certain wise minister said, "In the course of government, the rectification of disorder is like untying a knotted rope. It must not be done hurriedly. One must examine the knot carefully, then undo it."

The Path of Buddhahood is also like this. Having thoroughly understood its principles, one should practice them. As for those who thoroughly understand the methods of teaching, it is always those who have a powerful aspiration who can understand well. No matter how intelligent or brilliant one may be, one without the mind for the Way, who cannot detach from his ego and cannot forsake name and profit, will not become one of the people of the Path, nor will he understand the true principle.

2

He instructed,

People who study the Way should not study the Buddhist Teaching for the sake of their own egos. The Buddhist Teaching should be studied only for its own sake. The basic reality of this is that one must cast off his own body and mind, retaining nothing, and give it over to the vast ocean of the Buddhist Teaching. After that, without being concerned with any right or wrong, without maintaining personal attitudes, even if it be something difficult to do or hard to bear, in the service of the Buddhist Teaching one should force oneself to do it. And even if it is something that one insistently wants to do, whatever would not accord with the principles of the Buddhist Teaching should be abandoned. Do not hope to obtain good results as a reward for the merits of the Buddhist Way. Once having gone over to the Way of Buddhahood, think no more of yourself, but just continue to act in accordance with the rules of the Buddhist Teaching, and do not harbor personal prejudices. All our predecessors were thus. When the heart seeks nothing, it is at peace.

Even among people of the world, those who do not mix with others and grow up only in their own houses, who act as their hearts desire, considering their own wishes foremost, who are heedless of the views of others and who do not take into account the feelings of others, they are always bad. Concentration on the study of the Way is also like this. Joining in the congregation, obeying the teacher without insisting upon your own views, if you continue to reform your minds, you will easily become people of the Path.

In the study of the Way, one must first learn poverty. Abandoning fame, forsaking profit, free from all flattery, if you give up myriad concerns, you will not fail to become worthy men of the Way. In China, those who were known even to others as good monks were all poor people. Their clothes were tattered and their means were meager.

In former days the recorder[1] of the monastery on Mt. T'ien T'ung, a man called Senior Tao-ju, was the son of a prime minister. However, since he had left his family and relatives and had no lust for worldly gain, his clothing was so ragged that it was hard to look at; nevertheless, he was known as a man of virtue in the Way and even became the recorder of a great temple on a famous mountain.

Once I asked Senior Tao-ju, "As the son of an official, you are of a wealthy and high ranked family: why is everything about you so shabby and so poor?"

Senior Tao-ju replied, "Because I have become a monk."

3

ONE DAY HE INSTRUCTED,

A layman has said, "A treasure is an enemy that can harm one's body. In the past this was so, and it is so now as well."

This refers to a man of olden times who had a beautiful woman. At the time a powerful man asked for her, but the man was reluctant to part with her. Eventually the other man raised some troops and surrounded the house. As she was about to be taken, her husband said, "I am losing my life because of you."

The woman said, "I shall also lose my life for my husband." So saying, she fell from the high tower to her death. Subsequently her husband was spared, and lived to tell the story later.

Also there was once a wise man, who, as a provincial official, carried out the government of a province. At the time he had a son;

when this son took leave of his father to go on official business, his father gave him a bolt of fine silk.

His son said, "You are of high integrity; where did you get this silk?"

His father said, "It is left over from my salary."[1]

The son went to serve the emperor and reported this incident. The emperor was very much impressed by his wisdom. The son said, "My father has concealed his name, whereas I have revealed it. Truly the wisdom of my father is greater."

The meaning of this seems to be that although a single bolt of silk is a small quantity, a wise man does not take it for his personal use. Also a truly wise man hides his name. Since it was his official salary, he said that he would make use of it.

Even lay people are like this; how much more should the patch-robed ones studying the Path refrain from thinking of personal ends. Also, if one is devoted to the true Way, he should conceal his reputation as a man of the Way.

Once there was a wizard.[2] Someone asked him, "How can I learn wizardry?"

The wizard said, "If you want to learn wizardry, you must be devoted to the way of wizards."

Thus if students want to attain the Way of Buddhas and Patriarchs, they should be devoted to the Way of Buddhas and Patriarchs.

4

HE INSTRUCTED,

Of old there was a king, who, after pacifying the nation, asked all his ministers, "I govern the country well; am I really wise?"

The ministers said, "You govern very well; you are very wise."

But at the time one minister said, "You are not wise."

The king said, "Why?"

That minister said, "After ordering the nation, you gave it to your younger brother instead of your son."

This did not suit the sovereign's idea, so he drove the minister out. Afterwards he again asked another minister, "Am I benevolent?"

The minister said, "You are very benevolent."

The sovereign said, "Why?"

The minister said, "A benevolent ruler always has loyal ministers. Loyal ministers speak forthright words. That former minister was very forthright; he was a loyal servant. If you were not a benevolent ruler, you wouldn't have had one like him."

The king was impressed by this and recalled the former minister.

Also, in the time of the first emperor of Ch'in,[1] his crown prince said he was going to enlarge his flower park. A minister said, "Great! When the park is enlarged and many birds and beasts are gathered there, can we use those birds and beasts to hold off the armies of the neighboring countries?"

Because of this, the project was abandoned.

Also he said he was going to build a palace and lacquer its pillars. The minister said, "So it should be. When the pillars are lacquered, will our enemies desist?"

Thus that project too was stopped. The essence of Confucian teaching was to use skillful words in this way to put a stop to what was bad and encourage what was good. The tact of a patchrobed one in teaching others should also embody this spirit.

5

ONE DAY A MONK ASKED, "How does a wise one who lacks the mind of the Way compare to one without wisdom who has the mind of the Way?"

Dogen replied, "In many cases those without wisdom who have the mind of the Way eventually fall back. As for those who have wisdom, though they may be lacking in the mind of the Way, eventually they arouse the mind for the Way. Even in the present day there are many examples to prove this. Thus from the outset one should make the effort to study the Way without discussing whether or not he has the mind of the Way.

"If you study the Way, you ought to be poor. In reading the Inner and Outer writings, there were those who were poor, without place of abode; one drowned in the waters of Ts'ang Liang,[1] some hid on Mt. Shou Yang,² some sat on open ground under the trees or built huts in graveyards or deep in the mountains. Then again, there were also those who built palaces adorned with crimson lacquer and burnished gold and jewels. Both kinds are recorded in the classics. However, in exhorting those of later generations, they all consider poverty and lack of possessions to be fundamental. In admonishing wrong behavior, they criticize the rich as people of extravagance.

6

HE INSTRUCTED,

People who have left home should never rejoice upon receiving the offerings of others; yet do not refuse them either. The late high priest Eisai said, "To rejoice in the offerings of others is contrary to the Buddhist precepts. Not to rejoice offends the feelings of the donor."

The appropriate way to consider this is that it is not offered to me myself, but it is offered to the Three Treasures. Therefore, in reply, one should say "The Three Treasures shall surely accept this offering."

7

HE INSTRUCTED,

Of old it has been said that though a nobleman's power is greater than that of an ox, yet he does not contend with an ox.

Now you students, though you may think that our wisdom, talent, or learning may exceed others, do not indulge in disputation with other people. And do not chastise others with harsh words, or look at others with angry eyes.

Although people these days donate much wealth and offer support, due to displays of anger and slander by vicious words, there surely arise feelings of opposition.¹

Once upon a time master Chen Ch'ing K'o Wen² said to his community, "In the old days, when I was friends with Hsueh Feng Tao

Yuan in studying the Way, once Hsueh Feng was discussing the doctrine with a fellow student; in the dormitory they debated in loud voices, eventually coming to harsh words and argument. When the dispute had ended, Hsueh Feng said to me, 'You and I are fellow students of like mind; our bond is not shallow. Why did you not say anything when I was arguing with that other fellow?' At the time I only folded my hands, fearing to speak.

"Later, he became a teacher in one region, and I too am now an abbot. What I thought back then was that Hsueh Feng's discussion was after all useless. How much the more is it certainly wrong to argue. Since I thought it was useless to contend, I remained silent."

Students now should consider this well. If you are determined to work at studying the Way, you should value time to study the Way: what leisure time is there to engage in disputation? After all it is of no benefit to oneself or others.

This is so even for the Teaching; how much less should one engage in useless argument over worldly affairs! Although a nobleman's power exceeds that of even an ox, he does not contend with oxen. Though you may think you understand the doctrine better than another you should not try to defeat him in argument.

If there is a truly genuine student of the Way who asks about the Teaching, do not begrudge it to him, but expound it for him. However, even in that case, you should reply once after being questioned three times. Do not talk a lot or speak idly.

Ever since I read these words of Chen Ch'ing, I realized that I certainly had this fault too, and that he was admonishing me; therefore, I have thenceforth never disputed about doctrines with anyone else.

8

HE INSTRUCTED,

Many of the Ancients said, "Do not pass the time in vain." They also said, "Do not spend time idly." Now people who are studying the Way should value even a moment of time. This dewlike life quickly vanishes, time passes swiftly: while you live for even a little while, do not be concerned with other matters—you should only study the Way.

People these days say that their debt of gratitude to their parents is difficult to abandon, or they say that it is difficult to go against the will of their masters, or they say that it is difficult to leave their wives, children, and families, or that it would be difficult to assure the livelihood of their families, or they say that the people of the world would criticize them, or they say that they are poor and would be unable to get together the proper accoutrements, or they say that they are not of suitable capacity, incapable of studying the Way.

In this way they make emotional considerations, unable to leave their parents and masters, unable to abandon their wives, children, and dependents. As long as they go along with worldly feelings and covet property and wealth, they will pass their whole lives in vain and will surely regret it when they come to the end of their lives.

You should sit quietly and consider the truth and quickly determine to arouse the mind of the Way. Neither master nor parents can give one enlightenment; not wife, children, nor family can save one from suffering. Property and wealth cannot cut off one's revolving birth and death, nor can people of the world be of any help. If you claim you are not fit and do not practice, in what aeon will you attain enlightenment? You should just cast off myriad concerns and single-mindedly study the Way. Do not think about any later time.

9

HE INSTRUCTED,

In studying the Way, you must detach from your ego. Even if you have learned a thousand scriptures and ten thousand commentaries, if you do not get away from attachment to self, eventually you will fall into a pit of demons.

An Ancient said, "Without having the body and mind of the Buddhist Teaching, how can one become a Buddha or Patriarch?" What we call detachment from the self means to cast one's body and mind into the great ocean of the Buddhist Teaching, and to practice in accord with the Buddhist Teaching even though you may suffer painfully.

Though you may think that if you beg for food, people will think this is bad and unseemly; as long as you are thinking in this manner, you cannot by any means enter into the Buddhist Teaching. You should forget about all of the emotional views of society; just rely on the truth and study the Path. Considering the capacities of one's own body, to think that it would not be suitable for the Buddhist Teaching is also because one keeps clinging to self. To be concerned with the views of others and defer to people's feelings is the root of selfish clinging. Just study the Buddhist Teaching; do not follow worldly feelings.

10

ONE DAY EJO ASKED, "What is the course of activity of monastic study?"

Dogen said, "It is sole devotion to sitting. Whether upstairs or downstairs, cultivate stable concentration, without joining in the conversations of others; like a deaf and dumb man, you should always prefer to sit in solitude."

11

ONE DAY AFTER INTERVIEWS, HE INSTRUCTED,

Ta Tao Ku Ch'uan said, "I sit in the wind and sleep in the sun; it is better than to wear brocade like people these days."

Although these are the words of one of the Ancients, I have a little doubt about them. Does "people these days" refer to worldly covetous people? If so, he is attacking the pettiest of enemies. How are they even worthy of mention?

On the other hand, does it refer to people studying the Way? If so, then why does he say what he does is better than wearing brocade? As I look into his state of mind, it seems as though he may still attach some feeling of importance to brocade.

A sage is otherwise: whether gold and jewels or tiles and pebbles, he does not cling to them just the same. Therefore the Shakyan

Tathagata ate the cowmaid's milk boiled gruel[1] when he got it, and he also ate horse fodder[2] when he got it; he considered both equal.

There is no lesser or greater truth; there are the shallow and the deep among people. In the present age, give gold and jewels to some people and they will consider them valuable and will not take them; but something like wood or stone they would consider cheap and would accept and prize it. Gold and jewels originally come from the earth; wood and stone also originally are born of the earth: why avoid one because it is supposedly valuable and like the other because it is supposedly cheap? In considering this attitude, is it that there would be attachment in acquiring precious objects? If there is also a liking for what is cheap, the fault must be the same. This is something for students to be wary of.

12

HE INSTRUCTED,

When my late master Myozen was about to go to China,[1] his original master, Myoyu Acarya,[2] became gravely ill and was collapsed upon a sickbed, about to die.

At that time his master said to Myozen, "I am already old and sick, and my death is imminent; this time please put off going to China for a while, and help me in the sickness of old age: conduct me on the road of darkness,[3] and after I have died and gone, then you can fulfill your original intention."

Then my late master gathered Horui and his other disciples to discuss the matter with them. He said, "Since the time of my youth,[4] when I left my parents' home, I have received the support of this teacher and am now grown to maturity. My gratitude for his support and guidance is most profound. Even the fact that I learned the greater and lesser, temporary and true verbal Teachings of the transmundane doctrine, understood cause and effect, knew right from wrong, surpassed my colleagues and attained reknown, and also the fact that, knowing the truth of the Buddhist Teaching, I now have become determined to go to China to seek the Way, is all due solely to the benevolence of this teacher.

"But now he is already very advanced in years, and is prostrate on the bed of mortal illness. It is hard to say whether he has much life left and a reunion is not to be expected. Therefore he is trying to make me stay. It is hard to go against my master's will. Even my going to China now, mindless of my bodily life, in order to seek the truth, is for the sake of the bodhisattva's great compassion in helping sentient beings. Is there reason to go against the command of my master and go to China, or not? Let each of you express what he thinks."

At that point, several disciples all said, "You should give up the trip to China for this year. Your master's final illness is already critical; it is certain that he will die. If you stay just for this year and go to China next year, you will neither go against your master's will, nor be heedless of your debt of gratitude. Now even if you get to China a year or six months later, how will that hinder you? You will not violate the ideal of the master-disciple relationship, and your original intent to go to China will be as you wish."

At that time, as the youngest, I said, "If your understanding of the Buddhist Teaching is now already as you think it should be, then you should stay."

My late master said, "So it is. My practice of the Buddhist Teaching ought to be up to this: if I always keep on this way, I think I should attain the way to release."

I said, "If that is the case, then you should stay."

Then when everyone had given their approval, the late master Myozen said, "In your judgement, each of you gives only reasons why I should stay. My thought is otherwise. Since Myoyu is sure to die, even if I stay this time, his pain and suffering will not end because I have stayed and nursed him in his illness. Also it is not true that he could be released from birth and death because I propitiate him at the very end.[5] It would just be a matter of following his command for the moment to ease my master's mind. This is utterly useless for his release and attainment of the Way. If I were to let him wrongly hinder my aspiration to seek the truth, it would even be a cause of wrongdoing. However, fulfilling my aspiration to go to China to seek the truth, if I were to attain a degree of enlightenment, even though I go against one person's deluded feelings of attachment, yet I could become a factor in the realization of the Way for many people.[6] If the virtue of this accomplishment is more excellent, then it will have also requited my debt of gratitude to my teacher. Even if I were to die while crossing the sea and fail to fulfill my original intention, if I died with the aspiration to seek the truth, this desire would not come to an end life after life.[7] Think of the example of the Canonical Master Hsuan Tsang.[8] To vainly pass time, which is so easily lost, for the sake of one person, cannot be in accord with the will of the Buddhas. Therefore I have determined once and for all to go to China this time." And so he eventually went to China.

It was for such reasons that I thought my master had a truly genuine mind for the Way. Therefore you students now should not do anything useless and purposelessly waste time, whether supposedly for the sake of your parents, or for your teachers. Do not put off the Path of Buddhahood, which excels all other paths; do not pass the time in vain.

[At that time, Ejo said,]

"The reason why the conditional hindering factors of gratitude and affection for parents and teachers should be wholly abandoned for the sake of the search for real truth, is just as you say. However, even if one completely forsakes things like gratitude and love for parents and teachers, still when one considers the behavior of bodhisattvas, should one put aside one's own benefit and consider first the benefit of others? In this case, however, his old teacher's illness was serious, and with no one else to help him, luckily there was one person, Myozen, his protege, to take the responsibility. In that situation, if he thinks only of his own practice and does not help him, that seems to be contrary to the behavior of a bodhisattva. But one should not disdain the benevolence of a noble being. Should we consider the Buddhist Teaching according to circumstances, in actual situations? Going by such reasoning, should he have still stayed and helped? How could he only think of seeking the truth and not help his sick old teacher? What about this?"

[Dogen replied,] "Whether acting to help others or acting for one's own benefit, if one just gives up the lesser and takes the greater, this would be the benevolent action of a noble being. To live a frugal life of filial piety in order to help the sickness of old age is only the temporary happiness of illusory affection and deluded feelings in this life. If one turns away from the contrivance of deluded emotions to study the Uncontrived Way, even if there be some lingering resentment, it would be a superior help to leaving the world. Consider this.''

13

ONE DAY HE INSTRUCTED,

Worldly people often say, ''Though I have heard the words of such-and-such a teacher, it does not agree with my thoughts.''

These words are wrong. I do not know what is in their minds. Is it that the principle of the Sage's Teachings goes against their ideas, so they think it is wrong? This is total foolishness. Or is it that the teacher's words do not accord with their own ideas? If so, then, why ask a teacher anything to begin with? Or is it that this is said on the basis of habitual emotional views? If so, they are false ideas that have been held from beginningless past.

The attitude needed to study the Path is that even if they go against one's own ideas, if they are the words of one's teacher, or the stated principles of the Sage's Teachings, one should follow them completely, and abandon one's original personal opinions. This mind is the foremost requirement of the study of the Way.

In the past, there was one among my companions who went to his teacher clinging to his own views. Whatever did not agree with his ideas he claimed he didn't understand, and whatever conformed to his own views he held on to; thus he passed his whole life in vain and never understood the Buddhist Teaching.

Seeing him, I realized that the study of the Path should not be that way; so considering, I obeyed my master's words completely, and understood the principle thoroughly: after that, as I read the scriptures, one scripture said, ''If you want to study the Buddhist Teaching, do not keep continuing the mind of past, present, and future.''[1] I knew in truth that one must continue to reform step by step, without keeping in mind one's various past thoughts or former views. In a book it says, ''True words offend the ear.''[2] What this means is that words which would truly apply to oneself will always offend one's ears. Even though they offend, if one willfully follows and practices them, after all, there should be benefit.

14

ONE DAY IN THE COURSE OF A TALK on various subjects, he said,

There is fundamentally no good or bad in the human mind. Good and bad arise according to circumstances. For example, when someone's mind is aroused to enter into the mountain forests, he feels that the forest is good and human society is bad. Yet when he becomes bored and leaves the mountain forests, he feels that the forest is bad.

Thus it is that the mind definitely has no fixed characteristics; depending on circumstances, it may turn out any way at all. Therefore, when meeting good conditions the mind becomes good, and if it comes in the presence of bad conditions the mind becomes bad. Do not think that your mind is basically bad; you should just follow good conditions.

15

HE ALSO SAID,

It seems that people's minds surely go along with the words of others. In the *Ta Chih Tu Lun*[1] it says, "It is like a fool carrying a wishing jewel[2] in his hands. Someone sees him and says, 'You are really low down to be carrying something in your own hands.' Hearing this, he thinks, 'The jewel is precious, but reputation is a serious matter; I must be low down.' Worried about it, yet drawn only by reputation, he goes along with that other person's words; by deciding to put the jewel down to let someone else take it, in the end he loses the jewel."

Such is man's mind. Although one may think these words must surely be for one's own benefit, nevertheless, it may happen that he is hindered by his reputation and does not follow them. Then again, there are those who would go along with something for the sake of their reputation even while thinking it would certainly be bad for them.

When one goes along with what is good or bad, the heart is drawn by good and bad. Therefore, no matter how bad your heart may be originally, if you follow a good teacher and become familiar with good people, your heart also will naturally become good. If you approach evil people, though in the beginning you may think they are bad, eventually you will go along with their ideas, and to the extent that you become familiar with them, you will gradually become truly evil without realizing it.

Also, though a person may think in his mind that he will absolutely not let another take something from him, if the other asks for it insistently, he will give it even though he feels resentful and ill used. Then again, though one may definitely want to give it, if there is no opportunity, or the appropriate time has passed by, it may happen that he gives up the idea.

Thus even if students do not have a mind for the Way, having come near a good man, and having encountered favorable conditions, they should see and hear the same thing time and time again. Do not think that once you have heard these words you needn't listen to them any more. Even for those who have once aroused a mind for the Way, though it be the same thing, every time they hear about it their hearts will be polished and they will progress more and more. Even those who have not the mind of the Way, though one or two times it will make no impression on them, if they hear about it time and time again, just like when walking through dew and mist one's clothes become damp without one realizing when they have gotten wet, if you hear the words of a good man many times, feelings of shame will arise naturally and the true mind of the Way will also appear.

Therefore, once having understood, you should read the Sage's Teachings many times. And having heard the words of the teacher, still you should listen to them again. The mind should grow deeper and deeper. As for things which would be hindrances to the study of the Way, do not go near them anymore. Even if it is painful and lonely, associate with worthy companions to practice the Way.

16

HE INSTRUCTED,

Once when the meditation master Ta Hui[1] had an abscess on his buttock, a doctor looked at it and said it was serious. Ta Hui said, "If it is serious, will I die or not?"

The doctor said, "It is quite dangerous."

Ta Hui said, "'If I'm going to die, then all the more should I sit and meditate." As he still forced himself to sit, the abscess burst and came to naught.

The minds of the Ancients were like this; when they suffered illness they sat and meditated even more. People now should not lighten up on sitting meditation when they are not sick.

It seems that illness changes along with the mind. Ordinarily when someone has the hiccups, if you make some false accusation that calls for an apology, he will worry about it, and while he is trying to say something in his own defense, having forgotten about his hiccups, they have stopped. When I was going to China, on the boat, I was afflicted with diarrhea; but when a violent wind arose and there was turmoil in the boat, I forgot about my sickness, and it ceased.

Considering these examples, it seems that if one studies the Path diligently and forgets about other things, no illness should arise either.

17

HE INSTRUCTED,

A proverb says, "Unless you are deaf and dumb, you cannot be the master of the house."

What this means to say is that if one does not hear the slander of others and does not voice disapproval of others, he can succeed in his own task. Such a person is to be the master of the house.

Although this is a common proverb, you should take it and apply it to the conduct of a patchrobed monk. Without taking notice of the slander of others, without paying heed to the resentment of others, without expressing approval or disapproval of others, consider how you will travel the Path. Only those who have pierced the bone through the marrow can accomplish this.

18

HE INSTRUCTED,

The meditation master Ta Hui said, "The study of the Way should be done in the frame of mind of one who owes ten million strings of cash at the time when he is penniless but being pressed for payment. If you have such a mind, it is easy to find the Way.''

The *Hsin Hsin Ming*[1] says, ''The Supreme Way is without difficulty; just avoid picking and choosing.'' If you just cast off your picking and choosing mind, you would immediately realize this. To cast off the picking and choosing mind means to be detached from self. Do not think of studying the Buddhist Teaching in order to gain some advantage as a reward for practicing the Buddha's Teaching; you should only practice the Buddhist Teaching for the sake of the Buddhist Teaching itself. Even if you have learned a thousand scriptures and ten thousand commentaries, and have sat upon your meditation seat till it has worn out, without this mind you cannot find the Way of Buddhas and Patriarchs. You should only abandon body and mind, entrusting them to the Buddhist Teaching; following along with the others, when you no longer maintain your former views, you will then attain realization.

19

HE INSTRUCTED,[1]

In the *Spring and Autumn Annals*[2] it says, ''The fact that stone is hard means that even if you break it, you cannot take away its hardness. The fact that cinnabar is red means that even if you rub it, you cannot take away its redness.''

Once when a monk asked Hsuan Sha, ''What is the enduring body of reality like?'' Hsuan Sha said, ''Dripping with pus.''[3]

It seems that these basically have the same meaning.

20

HE INSTRUCTED,

An Ancient said, ''Take whatever goods and grain there are in store and entrust them to directors of affairs[1] who understand cause and effect; dividing the responsibility and distributing the authority, let them take charge of this.''

What this means is that the master has nothing at all to do with matters great or small pertaining to the monastic institution.² That is because his only work is to sit, to exhort and encourage the community.

It is also said, ''Even a thousand acres of clear fields is not as good as a meager skill that you can take around with you.''

''Bestowal of favor does not hope for reward; having given to someone, do not regret it.''

''If you keep your mouth as silent as your nose, you will avoid ten thousand calamities.''

''When one's behavior is noble, people naturally esteem him; when one's ability is great, people naturally submit to him.''³

''To plow deep but plant shallow is the way to a natural disaster. When you help yourself and harm others, how could there be no consequences?''

When students of the Way are looking at sayings, you must exert your power to the utmost and examine them very very closely.

21

HE INSTRUCTED,

An Ancient said, ''Atop a hundred foot pole, you should still advance another step.''¹

What this means is that you should be like one who has climbed to the top of a hundred foot pole, yet lets go his hands and feet, thus throwing down his body and mind.

There are several stages to this task. People these days appear to flee society and leave their homes, but when you consider their behavior, it is still not the escape from society of a leaver of home. One who is to be called a leaver of home must first give up his self, honor, and gain. Unless you are detached from these, even if you practice the Way with the urgency of beating out flames on your head² and your zeal is such that you may cut off your hands and feet,³ it will only be useless toil, not escape.

Even in China, although there are people who leave behind love and gratitude, which are so hard to part with, give up worldly wealth, which is hard to abandon, join the monastic communities and pass through the halls of the Patriarchal Teaching, there are also those who uselessly pass their whole lives in vain, without awakening to the Path or illumining their minds, just because they are acting without thorough knowledge of this basic truth.

The reason for this is that although in the beginning people's minds arouse an aspiration for the Way and they even become monks and follow a teacher, they do not think of becoming Buddhas or Patriarchs, but want word of their high status and the greatness of their own temple to be known to donors and patrons, to have it spoken of to family and dependents, to be honored and supported by others: some go on to contrive a pretext to have it said or thought that all the monks are corrupt and no good, whereas, "I alone have the mind of the Way, I am a good man."

People like this are as worthless of mention as evil monks like the Five Incorrigibles.[4] Theirs is a mental disposition bound for hell. Unknowing lay people think these are people with the mind of the Way, people worthy of esteem.

And there are those who go somewhat beyond this, who do not want donors or patrons, but join monastic communities and practice the Way; but those who are by nature basically lazy sluggards, because of the fact that they are actually being lazy, when the Great Elder or chief monk or someone is looking, make a show of practicing the Way; when they are not looking, there are those who laze around and idle away the time with anything handy. This is better than being so irresponsible in the householding life, but it is still not abandonment of selfish ego.

Also there are those who take no account of the ideas of their teachers, do not care whether the head monks or the brethren are looking or not; they always think, "The Way of Buddhahood is not for others; it is for myself alone. It is my body and mind that are to become a Buddha and a Patriarch." So they really work and strive. Although they seem as though they are more genuine people of the Path than those mentioned previously, still, because they practice for the betterment of their own selves, they are still not free from ego.

Even if you wish Buddhas and Bodhisattvas to rejoice over you and want to perfect enlightenment, the fruit of Buddhahood, it is because you have still not been able to give up your mind full of selfish desires for fame and profit. Up to this point, you have not left the hundred foot pole; you are clinging to it.

Only when one has cast body and mind into the Buddhist Teaching and practices it with no further hope of anything—even that he awaken to the Path and grasp the truth—such is called an Undefiled Wayfarer. This is the meaning of the saying, "Do not stay where there is Buddha; run quickly by where there is no Buddha."

22

HE INSTRUCTED,

Do not plan ahead what you will do for food and clothing. If you are completely out of food, then when it comes to that, you may beg for food. But if you plan to approach specific persons with your need, that is the same as storing something up, which is food obtained by improper means of livelihood.

As for the patchrobed ones, it is those who are like clouds, having no fixed abode, flowing onward like a stream, attached to nothing, who are called true monks.

Even if you do not have a single thing besides robe and bowl, if you depend upon a single patron, or rely upon your relatives, then yourself and others are bound fast; this is impure food. With a body and mind nourished and maintained by such impure food, even if you want to realize the pure and clean truth of all Buddhas, you will not be fit for it. Just as something died in indigo becomes blue and something died in yellow plum becomes yellow, so a body and mind stained by food obtained by improper livelihood is a body living wrongly. If you aspire to the Way of Buddhas with this body and mind, that would be like pressing sand to get oil.

You should just see to it that you may accord with this principle however you can as the occasion arises. Any forethought or provision beforehand is all wrong. You should consider this carefully.

23

HE INSTRUCTED,

Each student should know that everyone has great faults; and pride is the greatest fault. Both Buddhist and other books alike admonish this.

A secular classic says, "Although there are those who are poor but not obsequious, there are none who are rich but not proud," still restraining the wealthy, hoping that they will not be proud. This is certainly an important matter; you should think carefully about it.

When someone whose own status is low does not want to be inferior to people of high nobility, but wants to be superior to others, this is a case of extreme arrogance. Nevertheless, it is easy to admonish. But in the case of someone who has an ample share of worldly wealth of his own, his family surrounds him and others indulge him. Because he thinks this is right and is proud of it, downtrodden bystanders, seeing this, would become envious and bitter. How can someone who is himself rich and high class guard against the bitterness of others? A person like this is hard to admonish; he cannot restrain even his own person. And even if there is no pride in his heart, when he acts as he pleases, the downtrodden around him would be bitterly jealous. To restrain this is called restraining pride. To accept one's own wealth as a reward, without fearing the jealousy of the poor and downtrodden who see this, is called a proud heart.

A secular classic says, "Do not ride past a poor house in a chariot." Thus, even if it is appropriate to one's status to ride in a vermillion chariot, one should hesitate to do so in front of poor people.

The Buddhist classics are also like this. However, student monks now want to excel others by way of wisdom and learning. Under no circumstances should you be proud of these. To talk about the wrongs of one's inferiors, or knowing the wrongs of one's forebears or colleagues and slandering them, is extreme arrogance. An Ancient said, "Though you be defeated in the presence of the wise, do not excel in the presence of fools." Even if others have wrongly understood something which I myself know quite well, if I were to speak of their errors, that would also be my own error. Even if you talk about the Teachings, do not slander your predecessors or senior colleagues; and in situations where ignorant and unenlightened people might be resentful and jealous, consider this carefully.

When I was staying in Kennin Temple, many people asked about the Teaching. Among them were many wrong interpretations and mistakes; but thinking deeply of this proper conduct, I just spoke of the virtues of the Teaching as they are and did not discuss the wrongs of others and ended up without trouble. The depth of grasping views of the ignorant is such that they would surely have become angry, saying that I had mentioned the faults of their worthy predecessors. For a man endowed with wisdom to be truly genuine, once he just knows the principle of the Buddhist Teaching, then without anyone saying anything, he realizes and corrects his own mistakes and those of his worthy forebears. You should think on and understand such matters as this.

24

HE INSTRUCTED,

In the study of the Way, the prime essential is sitting meditation. The attainment of the Way by many people in China is due in each case to the power of sitting meditation. Even ignorant people with no talent, who do not understand a single letter,[1] if they sit wholeheartedly in meditation, then by the accomplishment of meditative stability, they will surpass even brilliant people who have studied for a long time. Thus, students should only be concerned with the act of sitting; do not get involved with other things. The Way of Buddhas and Patriatchs is just sitting meditation; one should not follow other concerns.

[At that time Ejo asked,] "In practicing both sitting and reading, when looking at the recorded sayings and public cases,[2] it happens that one may understand somewhat one out of a hundred or a thousand. In the case of sitting meditation, there is no such particular experiential proof as this. Yet should we still be devoted to sitting meditation?"

[Dogen replied,] "When looking at the words of the public cases, though one seems to have some perception, that is a factor which causes estrangement from the Way of Buddhas and Patriarchs. If you spend your time sitting upright without attaining anything or understanding anything, then this would be the Way of Buddhas and Patriarchs. Although even the Ancients encouraged both reading and sole occupation with the act of sitting, they still encouraged sitting wholeheartedly. And though there have been people whose awakening was opened by words, they too were situations in which the opening of awakening was due to accomplishment in sitting. The true attainment is due to the sitting.''

NOTE TO 1

1. Kao Tsu (reigned 206–195 B.C.) was the founder of the Former Han dynasty (206 B.C.–8 A.D.).

NOTE TO 2

1. The recorder (Japanese *shoki*) is in charge of writing all the official notices, letters, etc., in the course of temple affairs; according to ancient standards, this important office is to be filled by an outstanding monk who is also accomplished in calligraphy and skilled in the use of language.

NOTES TO 3

1. Silk and grain were standard media for taxes and official salaries in China and Japan.
2. *Sennin*; this refers to practitioners of Taoist occult arts. This term is sometimes translated as ''Immortal,'' since the avowed aim of many of these occultists was immortality or longevity. However, the term includes people who practiced all sorts of magic and sorcery and developed supernormal powers.

NOTE TO 4

1. Ch'in Shih Huang Ti (r. 246–210 B.C.), first emperor of the Chinese empire.

NOTES TO 5

1. This refers to Ch'u Yuan; see book II, section 23.
2. This refers to two brothers, Po I and Shou Ch'i, who were heirs to a feudal kingdom under the ancient Shang (Yin) dynasty in China (ca. eighteenth–thirteenth century B.C.). When King Wu of Chou overthrew the Shang in 1122 B.C., these two brothers condemned his clan as rebels and fled into Mt. Shou Yang, where they starved to death. They are classical exemplars of loyalty from the Confucian point of view.

NOTES TO 7

1. Perhaps this refers to the intensifying sectarian disputes of the day, intimately connected as they were to the material and political fortunes of the various sects.
2. Chen Ch'ing K'o Wen (1025–1102) and Hsueh Feng Tao Yuan (n.d.) were both successors to the great master Huang Lung Hui Nan, the founder of the Huang Lung branch of Lin Chi Zen.

NOTES TO 11

1. In former days, the Buddha-to-be used to indulge in self-mortification and rigorous fasting to the point of emaciation; having at length resolved to abandon these extreme austerities as useless, the first food he was offered was rice boiled in the milk of cows fed on the milk of milk-fed cows: thus it represents very fine food, and is said to have immediately restored the Buddha's golden color.

2. This was one of the so-called "nine hardships" of the Buddha: once a brahmin king, Agnidatta, invited Buddha and five hundred of his disciples to Agnidatta's kingdom to pass the summer retreat. The king, however, had forgotten to provide food for them all; the master of the stables brought out half of the fodder of five hundred horses to offer to the congregation, and they lived on that for the summer.

NOTES TO 12

1. Myozen (1183–1225), leading disciple of Eisai, first taught Rinzai (Lin Chi) Zen to Dogen; later, in 1223, he accompanied Dogen to China for further study, dying there two years later.
2. Acarya, Sanskrit for "teacher," was used in Japan as a title for masters of the Shingon and Tendai sects. Myoyu was of the Tendai sect, and thus so was Myozen originally, as were Eisai and Dogen, and many others who later entered into the new religious movements of the twelfth and thirteenth centuries.
3. This refers to services to "transfer merit" to the dying and dead, to propitiate their well-being in future lives.
4. Myozen left his home and became Myoyu's protege when he was only eight years old; thus the extent of his debt to this teacher is hardly exaggerated.
5. This refers back to the death services; it is interesting to see that Myozen regarded these as ultimately useless. This is very much in the spirit of pristine Buddhism, which did not rely on ceremonies. Dogen also especially scorned those monks who worked as ceremonialists and chanters of charms for the rich and powerful.
6. In his capacity as an enlightened teacher.
7. This is illustrated by the fact that although Myozen did actually die in China, his disciple Dogen did succeed in becoming enlightened and brought the teaching back to Japan.
8. Hsuan Tsang (600–664) was probably the most famous of Chinese pilgrims and translators; he journeyed to India by the overland route, setting out in either 627 or 629, reached India in 633, traveled and studied extensively there, returned to China in 645, and spent the rest of his life translating Buddhist texts from Sanskrit to Chinese. He specialized in the teaching that there is only consciousness, and is the very model of an intrepid man.

NOTES TO 13

1. Literally, "the mind of the three worlds (ages)": this can refer to time, as it has been rendered here, according to the context, and it also can refer to the realms of desire, form, and formlessness.
2. From *Kung-tzu Chia Yu,* "Household sayings of Confucious"; it also appears in the *Kuei Shan Ch'ing Ts'e,* "Admonitions of Kuei Shan," previously quoted by Dogen, and doubtless reappears in many books.

NOTES TO 15

1. Mahaprajnaparamita Shastra, "Commentary on Perfection of Wisdom" ascribed to Nagarjuna (first-second century A.D.); translated by Kumarajiva (fl. 397–415) into Chinese, there is no Sanskrit original known to exist.
2. Sanskrit *cintamani,* a wish-granting jewel, sometimes used as a metaphor for mind.

NOTE TO 16

1. Ta Hui Tsung Kao (1089–1163) was a successor to the Yang-ch'i branch of the Lin Chi sect; many people considered him a great teacher, and most of the

teachers of Zen in Japan around Dogen's time were descended from Ta Hui. Sores are common with people who remain immobile for long periods of time; Bodhidharma, the First Patriarch of Zen in China, is popularly said to have lost his legs by not using them for nine years.

NOTE TO 18

1. This famous poem is attributed to Seng Ts'an (d. 606), the Third Patriarch of Zen in China. The lines Dogen quotes are the opening of the poem.

NOTES TO 19

1. This section is added following the Choenji book.
2. This is not the classic attributed to Confucius, but rather the *Lu Shih Shun Ch'iu,* a compendium of dissertations on various subjects of history, philosophy, law, war, etc. compiled by Lu Pu Wei of the Ch'in dynasty.
3. This is taken from the *Ta Hui Cheng Fa Yen Tsang,* a compendium of Zen stories made by the master Ta Hui mentioned in sections 16 and 18 above; the preface to the part quoted is that Hsuan Sha once mistakenly took some medicine and his whole body became inflamed. Hsuan Sha Shih Pei (835-908) was a successor of Hsueh Feng I Tsun, who appears in book VI, section 5.

NOTES TO 20

1. There were usually six offices charged with business and administrative duties.
2. That is, the teaching master has nothing to do with the property or finances of the monastery.
3. The Choenji book has it, "A man whose action is firm is naturally admired; but a man of outstanding ability will naturally be brought down."

NOTES TO 21

1. Ching Ts'en of Ch'ang Sha, in Hunan, was a successor of Nan Ch'uan (see book I, section 6): once he composed the following verse:

> The man immobile atop the hundred foot pole
> Has attained Entry, but is not yet Real.
> Atop the hundred foot pole, it is necessary to
>   step forward;
> The universe in the ten directions is his whole body.

A monk asked him, "Just when one is at the top of a hundred foot pole, how can he step forward?"
The master said, "The mountains of Liang province; the rivers of Li province."
The monk said, "Please tell me."
The master said, "All within the four seas and five lakes is under the Imperial Sway." (*Ching Te Ch'uan Teng lu* 10)
2. This is a classic metaphor for paying utmost attention to one's task. It appears in the *Kashyapaparivarta,* II.
3. In this rendering, I follow the Choenji edition; it seems reasonable that this could refer to the Second Patriarch of Zen cutting off his arm in the middle of winter. The *rufobon* has it "Your zeal is such that you know the 'raising of the leg.'" This refers to a story of the Buddha's bodhisattvahood, when he spent seven days reciting extemporaneous verses of praise of an ancient Buddha, forgetfully keeping his foot raised in the interim. The story comes from the *Mahaprajnaparamita Shastra.*

4. The five sandhilas, lazy monks who would do nothing but make a show of meditating, whereby to obtain the offerings of the ignorant devout; they eventually all
   went to hell and were reborn as imperfect beings such as eunuchs and barren
   women.

NOTES TO 24

1. According to the Choenji book; the *rufubon* has it, "who cannot understand (or
   ask) a single question."
2. *Koan*; incidents in the lives and sayings of Zen masters, later used as contemplation themes.

BOOK VI

1

He instructed,

If you must feel shame before people, you should feel shame before people who have enlightened eyes.

When I was in China, Master Ching of T'ien T'ung Monastery invited me to be his personal attendant. Saying, "Although Dogen is a foreigner, he is a man of capacity," thus, he invited me. I firmly declined. My reason was that although it would be an important thing, both for my reputation in Japan and for the purpose of study in learning the Way, yet as long as there were people among the congregations who possessed eyes, for a foreigner to be an attendant in a great monastery might be criticized for giving the appearance that there were no men in the great country of China. Thinking that I should exercise utmost deference, I expressed my idea in a letter. Master Ching heard it, and being impressed with esteem for the country and shame before others, he let me go and did not ask again.

2

He instructed,

Someone said, "I am sick, not a fit vessel, incapable of studying the Way. Having heard the essentials of the Teaching, I want to live alone in retirement, spending my life taking care of my body and nursing my sickness."

This is very wrong. The former sages did not necessarily have golden bones. Could the Ancients have all had superior capacities? When we consider the time since Buddha's death, it has not been so long; and thinking back to when he was in the world, not everyone was a genius. There were good people as well as bad ones. There were also those among the congregation of monks whose behavior was incredibly bad; and there those whose capacities were of the lowest sort. Nevertheless, there were none who demeaned themselves or said they would give up, thus failing to arouse the aspiration to the Way, none who failed to study the Way on the grounds that they were not fit vessels. If you do not study the Way and cultivate its practice in this life, in which life would you become a man of capacity, a man without illness, to study the Way? Just to arouse the mind and cultivate practice without worrying about your bodily life, this is the most essential thing in the study of the Way.

3

HE INSTRUCTED,

Students of the Way, do not covet food or clothing. Everyone has an allotment of food, an allotment of life; even if you seek food and livelihood that is not your own lot, you will not succeed in getting them. How much the more for those who study the Way of Buddha; there are the offerings of donors, food obtained from begging that will never run out, and then there are also permanent temple supplies. It is not a matter of private enterprise. Fruits, food obtained from begging, and donations from the faithful—these three kinds of food are all pure food. As for the other four kinds of food—from farming, commerce, war, and crafts—these are all impure, food from improper livelihood. They are not for the consumption of those who have left the householding life.

Long ago there was a monk who died and went to the Dark Road. Yama, the king of the dead, said, "This man's allotment of life is not yet exhausted; he should be sent back."

One of the ministers of darkness said, "Though his allotment of life is not yet exhausted, his allotment of food is already used up."

The king said, "Then let him eat lotus leaves."

Thenceforth, after that monk came back to life, he could not eat the food of humans, but maintained the life left to him eating only lotus leaves.

Thus, for leavers of home, due to the power of studying Buddha-hood, their allotment of food should not be exhausted. The single feature of the White Hair[1] and the twenty years of grace[2] left by the Buddha, though they be used for aeons, would never be exhausted. It just means that you should practice the Path single-mindedly and not seek food and clothing.

As long as the body, limbs, blood, and flesh are well kept, the mind, accordingly, will become well; we read this even in medical prescriptions. How much the more so for those who study the Way: if you maintain discipline and purity of behavior, regulating the body in accordance with the behavior of Buddhas and Patriarchs, then your mind, also, will accordingly be in tune.

Students of the Way, whenever you are about to speak, you should reflect thrice as to whether it would be of benefit for self and others; if it would be beneficial, then say it. Words with no benefit should be left unsaid. Even something like this is difficult to attain all at once. Keeping it in mind, you should practice it gradually.

4

DURING A TALK ON VARIOUS SUBJECTS, HE SAID,

Students of the Way, do not worry about food and clothing. Al-though Japan is a small country in an outlying area, in the past as well as present there have been many people who attained fame in the Exoteric and Esoteric schools, and who were known even to peo-ple in later generations. Also there have been many people accom-plished in the various fields of poetry, music, literary, and martial arts; among such people, I have never heard of even one who had abundant food and clothing. All of them endured poverty, forgot about other concerns, and devoted themselves wholeheartedly to their particular path; that is why they attained their fame.

How much the more does this apply to people studying the Way in the school of the Patriarchs; abandoning worldly occupation, they do not run after any fame or profit—how could they become rich? In the monasteries of the great country of China, although it is the Final Age [of Dharma], there are thousands and ten thousands of people studying the Way; among them are those who come from far away and those who come from the rural areas. In either case, most of them are poor. Nevertheless, they do not consider poverty an affliction. Troubled only by the fact that they have not yet awakened to the Way, they sit, whether upstairs or downstairs, and wholeheartedly practice the Buddha Way, as though mourning their dead parents.[1]

I personally witnessed the case of a monk from Ssu Ch'uan who had nothing since he had come from afar.[2] All he had was two or three sticks of ink,[3] worth about two or three hundred Chinese coins or about twenty or thirty Japanese coins: buying some cheap grade, extremely flimsy Chinese paper, he made upper and lower garments out of it; when he wore these, they would make a tearing sound as he stood and sat, but he did not take notice of his shabbiness, nor was he troubled by it. Someone said, "You should return to your native village and get a proper outfit together." He replied, "My native village is far away; I fear I would waste time on the journey and lose time in studying the Way." He even studied the Way without being troubled by the cold. Thus it is that good people appear in China.

5

He instructed,

I have heard that long ago when the moastery on Mt. Hsueh Feng[1] was founded, it was extremely poor; sometimes there was no food at all, and sometimes they steamed green beans with rice to eat, thus passing the days studying the Way; yet later there were never less than fifteen hundred monks there.

The people of old were like this; today they should also be like this. The deterioration of monkhood stems largely from wealth and honor. During Buddha's lifetime, Devadatta's jealousy[2] also arose from daily offerings of five hundred cartloads of provisions. He did not harm only himself, but also caused others to commit evil deeds. How could a genuine student of the Way become rich? Even if many offerings made in pure faith accumulate, you should think of your debt of gratitude and consider how you will repay it.

People in this country will even give out of consideration for their own benefit. To give generously to one who approaches with a smile is the established way of the world. But if you just do it so as to go along with the feelings of others, it would be a hindrance to the study of the Way. You should simply endure the hunger, endure the cold, and study the Way singlemindedly.

6

ONE DAY HE INSTRUCTED,

An Ancient said, "One must hear, one must see, one must attain."[1] He also said, "If you haven't attained, you should see; if you haven't seen, you should hear."

What this means is that seeing is better than hearing, and attaining is better than seeing. If you haven't yet attained, you must see; if you haven't yet seen, you must hear.

7

HE ALSO SAID,

The essential point in studying the Way is just to cast off your original attachments. If you first reform the comportment of your body, the mind also will reform along with it. If first you maintain the prescribed dignity and disciplined behavior, your mind too should accordingly reform.

In China, it is a popular custom for people to gather at their ancestral shrines and pretend to cry, as their offering of filial piety to their parents; while they are doing this, eventually they really do cry. People who study the Way too, though from the beginning they may not have the mind for the Way, if they would but insistently devote themselves to the study of the Way, eventually the true mind of the Way should arise.

Beginners in the study of the Way should just follow the community in practicing the Way. Do not think of learning and knowing such things as the essential points and ancient standards of practice right away. Things like those ancient standards and essential points are just something one should know thoroughly and correctly when about to enter the mountains alone or to conceal oneself within a city in order to practice. If you follow the congregation in your practice, you should attain the Way. For example, it is like riding in a boat; although you yourself may not know how to row, if you leave it to an able boatman to go along, whether you know anything or not, you will arrive at the other shore. If you follow a wise teacher and practice together with the community without any selfishness, you will naturally become a man of the Way.

Students of the Way, even if you attain enlightenment, do not think that this is now the ultimate and thus abandon your practice of the Way. The Way is endless. Even if you are enlightened, you should still practice the Way. Consider the ancient story of the lecturer Liang Sui calling upon Ma Yu.[1]

8

He instructed,

Students of the Way, do not think of waiting for a later day to practice the Way. Without letting this day and this moment pass by, just work from day to day, moment to moment.

A layman in these parts who had been sick for a long time made the following promise to me last spring: "If this present illness is cured I will definitely leave my wife and children, build a hut to live in near the temple, participate in the *uposatha* ceremony[1] twice a month, daily practice the Way, read and listen to discourse on the Teaching, and pass my life preserving disciplined behavior as best I can." Subsequently, since he took various curatives, his illness remitted somewhat, but he had a relapse, and passed days and months idly. Since January of this year, suddenly his condition became critical, and as his pain and suffering gradually overcame him, because he had not the time to bring the necessary equipment to build the hut he had been planning, therefore, he rented someone's room right off and stayed there, but within one or two months he had died and gone. In the meantime he had accepted the Bodhisattva Precepts and taken refuge in the Three Treasures, so he faced the end well; thus, it was better than to have stayed at home, hanging on to gratitude and love towards his wife and children, to die in mad confusion. Considering, however, that it would have been better had he left his home last year when the thought occurred to him, and approached the temple, become familiar with the monks, and ended his life practicing the Way, it seems to me that the cultivation of the Buddha Way is something that should not wait for a later time.

The thought that because the body is sick one will cultivate practice after healing the sickness, is one entertained by those who lack the mind for the Way. With bodies made of the compounding of elements, who would have no sickness? The Ancients did not necessarily have golden bones; it is just that once their determination was thoroughgoing, they forgot about other things in order to practice. When something critical comes up in life, one will inevitably forget about petty things. Since the Way of Buddhas is the One Great Concern, in hoping to complete it in one lifetime, you should determine not to waste the days and hours.

An Ancient said, "Do not pass the time in vain." While you are attempting to cure your illness, as long as it doesn't go away and the pain and suffering oppresses you more and more, you should determine to practice the Way when the pain has lightened a bit.[2] When you suffer severe pain, you should think to practice before it gets even worse. When it gets critical, you should think to practice before you die. In trying to cure disease, some get better and some get worse. And it also happens sometimes that it gets better even though you don't try to cure it, or it may get worse even though you try to cure it. You should consider this carefully.

People practicing the Way should not think they will practice the Way only after having prepared a dwelling place and gotten together their robes and bowls and such. While someone in the extreme of poverty is waiting to get together the robes, bowls, and implements which he lacks, what about the gradual approach of death? Therefore, if you wait for a place to stay and wish to practice the Way after having gotten together robes and bowl, you would pass your whole life in vain. Though you may not have robes and bowl, just think that even in the household life, the Buddha Way may be carried out and so you should practice it. This is also because robes and bowl are merely the proper trappings of monkhood; a true traveler on the Way of Buddhahood does not depend upon them. You shall have them as they become available; do not purposely seek after them. Neither should you decide not to have what you should have. Also, when you have an illness that needs to be cured, if you neglect to treat it, thinking that you would sooner die, this too is the view of a heretic. For the sake of the Buddha Way, do not be anxious for your life; yet do not be careless of it, either. If they are available, the use of moxa cautery or medicines wouldn't be a hindrance to the practice of the Way. But it is wrong to put off the study of the Way, thinking that curing the illness comes first, that only after that will you cultivate your practice.

9

He said,

In the sea there is a place known as the Dragon Gate,[1] where huge waves repeatedly rise. When fish have passed through this place, they always become dragons: therefore, it is called the Dragon Gate.

Now it seems to me that the waves there are no different from anyplace else and the water, too, is the same salt water. Nevertheless, it is an established miracle that when fish pass through there they always become dragons. The scales of the fish do not change and their bodies remain the same; yet suddenly they become dragons.

The form for the patchrobed ones is also like this. Though the place is not different from others, once they have entered the monastery, they will definitely become Buddhas and Patriarchs. They eat food and wear clothes like other people; though the relief from hunger and protection from the cold are the same, when they just shave off their hair, put on monk's garments, and eat gruel and vegetables for food, suddenly they become patchrobed ones. To become Buddhas and be Patriarchs is not a matter of seeking afar. The question of entering or not entering a monastery is the same as the difference between passing or not passing through that Dragon Gate.

Also there is a proverbial saying, "Though I sell gold, there is none to buy." The Way of Buddhas and Patriarchs is also like this; it is not that they begrudge the Way, but, although they are always offering it, people do not get it. Gaining the Way does not depend upon the sharpness or dullness of the faculties; everyone can awaken to the truth. Depending upon zeal or sloth, there is slowness or quickness in attaining the Way. The difference between zeal and sloth is whether one's determination is thoroughgoing or not. When one's determination is not thoroughgoing, it is because he does not contemplate impermanence. We die from moment to moment,[2] ultimately not abiding even for a while. As long as you are alive for the time being, do not pass the time in vain.

An ancient saying has it, "The rat in the storehouse hungers for food; the ox pulling the plow in the field hasn't his fill of grass." What this means is that one is hungry though in the midst of food, one lacks for grass while being in the middle of grass. People are also like this: though they are in the midst of the Buddha Way, they do not merge with the Way. If the mind which seeks fame and profit does not come to rest, one will be ill at ease all his life long.

10

HE INSTRUCTED,

The actions of a man of the Way, whether good or bad, all have some intent. They cannot be judged by ordinary people.

In olden times, the high priest Eshin[1] once had someone drive away a deer that was eating grass in the garden. At the time someone asked him, "The master seems to have no compassion: do you begrudge the grass, causing suffering to the animal?"

The high priest said, "No. If I didn't drive it away, this deer would eventually become used to human beings; should it encounter an evil man, it would surely be killed. Therefore I drive it away."

Although it seems merciless to drive away the deer, yet the profound reasoning of compassion within his inner heart was like this.

11

ONE DAY HE INSTRUCTED,

If someone asks about the Teaching, or asks about the essentials of the method of practice, a patchrobed monk should always reply on the basis of the truth. In case you perceive that another has not the capacity, or else you consider that as a beginner who has not yet learned anything, he would not be able to understand, still you should not answer him in terms of expedients that are not really true.

The intent of the Bodhisattva Precepts is that even if one with capacity for the Lesser Vehicle should ask about the path of the Lesser Vehicle, one should only reply to him in terms of the Greater Vehicle. The manner of the Buddha's lifetime-Teaching was also like this: the expedient temporary teachings are in reality without benefit; only the final true Teaching is of genuine benefit. Thus you should not discuss whether another will attain or not; just reply to him with the truth.

If you see these people, you should see them in terms of their real virtues; don't see them in terms of their outward appearance or contrived virtue.

In ancient times, there was a certain man who came and submitted to Confucius. Confucius asked him, "Why do you come submit to me?"

He said, "As I look upon you, noble man, in our interview, you have majestic dignity; that is why I submit to you."

Then Confucius ordered his disciples to bring out all his chariots, vestments, gold, silver, and other property; giving it all to the man, he said, "It is not me that you are submitting to," and he handed it over to him.

Once, when the regent of Uji[1] went to his bathhouse boiler room and saw the place where the fires are lit, the worker there saw him and said, "Who is this fellow who comes to the regent's boiler room without any notice?" And he chased him out.

After being chased out, the regent changed out of the poor clothes he had been wearing at first: when he appeared magnificently costumed, the aforementioned worker, seeing him from a distance, got scared and fled. At that point the regent hung up his costume on a pole and bowed to it. Someone asked him what he was doing. He replied, "The fact that I am esteemed by others is not because of my own virtues; it is just because of this costume."

This is the way fools respect others. Respect for the written words of the scriptural teachings is also like this.

An ancient said,[2] "Though his words fill the land, he is without fault of tongue; though his activity extend through the land, there is no harm from enmity.'' This is because he says what is to be said and does what is to be done. These are the words and speech of the essential path of ultimate virtue. As for worldly words and speech, when they are planned and carried out by personal prejudice, I fear that there may be nothing but wrong. The precedents for the speech and behavior of patchrobed monks have been established; you should not retain selfish prejudices. This is the Way which has been practiced by Buddha and Patriarchs.

Students of the Way must each examine their own selves. To examine oneself means that one must reflect upon how one should bear his own body and mind. But the patchrobed monks are already sons of the Buddha; they should develop the style of comportment of the Buddha. For the conduct of the body, mouth, and mind, there are manners that have been practiced by former Buddhas; each of you should follow those standards.

Even an ordinary man has said, ''One's clothes should conform to the law, one's speech should accord with the Way.''[3] How much more is this true for patchrobed monks; they should not exercise any selfishness at all.

12

He instructed,

When people studying the Way these days listen to the Teaching, since most of them primarily want it to be known that they have understood it well, and they want their replies to sound good, therefore the words they are hearing pass right by their ears. All this demonstrates is that they lack the mind of the Way, and retain their selfish egoism.

One must just first forget his own self, listen carefully to hear what others say; afterwards, think about it calmly, and if there is some difficulty or question, pursue it and criticize. If you have understood, you should again present your understanding to the teacher. If you make the claim of having understood on the spot, you have not really listened closely to the teaching.

13

HE INSTRUCTED,

During the reign of Emperor T'ai Tsung of T'ang, he was presented with a superlative steed by a foreign country. Having gotten this horse, the emperor said to himself without joy, "Even if I alone ride a thousand miles on a superb mount, without retainers to follow me, it would be pointless." Therefore he summoned Wei Ch'eng, and when he asked him about this, Ch'eng said, "I agree with the feelings of the emperor." Thus they loaded that horse with gold and cloth and sent it back.

Even a worldly sovereign did not keep something useless, but sent it back. How much the more does this apply to patchrobed monks; anything outside of robes and bowl is definitely useless. Why keep something useless? Even in the ordinary world, those who single-mindedly cultivate one path do not consider it necessary to possess such things as fields, gardens, or manors; they just consider all the people of the land to be their family and people.

Chiso, entitled "Bridge of Dharma," left his will to his son, saying, "You must only strive wholeheartedly on your path." How much the more should sons of Buddha abandon myriad concerns and cultivate one thing single-mindedly. This is the most important point to keep in mind.

14

HE INSTRUCTED,

Students of the Way, when you go to the teacher to ask about the doctrine, be most thoroughgoing; having asked, ask again and be completely sure. If you go by without asking what you should ask or saying what you should say, it would surely be a loss to you.

The teacher always awaits the questions of the disciple to say anything himself. Even things you understand, you should ask about again and again to make sure. The teacher too should ask the disciple whether he has understood, and should instruct him.

15

HE INSTRUCTED,

In the consideration of people of the Way, there is something different from that of ordinary people. When the late high priest of Kenninji [Eisai] was in the world, it happened that the temple ran completely out of food. At that time a donor asked Eisai [to accept] an offering of a bolt of silk. Eisai rejoiced and personally carried it back to the temple, not even having someone else carry it for him. He gave it to a director of affairs and said, "Use this to get tomorrow's gruel and so forth."

However, there came a request from the home of a certain layman, saying, "An embarrassing matter has come up, so that I need two or three bolts of silk; if you have anything at all please let me have it."

Eisai immediately took back the aforementioned silk and gave it to the layman. At this time the monk who was director of affairs, as well as the rest of the monks, were all exceedingly confounded.

Later, Eisai said, "You are all probably thinking it was wrong: but my thought was that the community of monks has gathered because they aspire to the Buddha-Way. Even if one day you have no food and die of starvation, it shouldn't bother you. When you save people in the world from their affliction of lacking what is needed, the benefit to everyone would be greater."

Truly the consideration of a man of the Way is like this.

16

HE INSTRUCTED,

The Buddhas and Patriarchs were all originally ordinary men. While they were ordinary men, they could not but have done bad things, had bad thoughts, been stupid, been foolish. Nevertheless, because they all changed, followed wise teachers, and cultivated practice, they all became Buddhas and Patriarchs.

You people now should be likewise. Do not demean yourselves, saying that you are stupid and dull. If you do not arouse your minds in this life, when will you ever practice the Way? If you now practice insistently, you should not fail to attain the Way.

17

HE INSTRUCTED,

A proverb about the guideline for the way of sovereigns says, "If the breast is not empty, it will not admit loyal words." What this means is that the way of sovereignty is practiced by following the words of loyal ministers, according to what is right, without maintaining one's own views.

The guideline for the concentration of patchrobed monks should also be like this. If you retain your own views in the slightest, the words of the teacher do not get through to you. If the teacher's words do not get through to you, you do not grasp the teacher's doctrine. It is not just a matter of forgetting about different views of the doctrine; when you have forgotten about worldly concerns, and such matters as hunger and cold, and thoroughly purified your body-mind to listen, then you will really be able to hear. When you listen in this way, the principle, as well as your uncertainties, become clarified. As for what is called true attainment of the Way, if you cast off your previous state of body and mind and just straightforwardly follow the teacher, then you become a true man of the Way. This is the foremost of ancient verities.

NOTES TO 3

1. See book IV, section 15, note 1.
2. This refers to the fact that Shakyamuni lived only eighty years out of an idealized lifetime of one hundred; the remaining twenty years he donated to future beings. This represents the life of the Buddhist community.

NOTES TO 4

1. Hsuan Sha Shih Pei once said, "If you have wisdom, you can gain release immediately, right now. If your faculties are slow and dull, then you must work hard, endure and forebear; day and night forgetting weariness and ignoring food, as though mourning your dead parents." (*Ching Te Chuan Teng lu,* 18)
2. Ssu Ch'uan is in western China, whereas Dogen studied for the most part in eastern China.
3. Chinese ink is made into sticks which can be ground in water for use.

NOTES TO 5

1. Hsueh Feng was opened by the reknowned Zen master I Ts'un (822–908) during the 870's, a period of tremendous civil strife within China, just prior to the fall of the three-century-old T'ang Dynasty. In spite of this, monks came from all over to study under I Ts'un and it is said that his community numbered as many

as seventeen hundred. I Ts'un had fifty-six enlightened disciples and was the Patriarch of both the Yun Men and Fa Yen sects of Zen.

2. Devadatta, cousin and one-time disciple of the Buddha, is typed as the arch-villain of early Buddhist history, charged with the three grievous crimes of shedding Buddha's blood, killing an Arhat, and disrupting the harmonious community of disciples. He enlisted king Ajatashatru as his own patron and set himself up in opposition to the Buddha.

NOTE TO 6

1. The Choenji version has "experience" for "attain."

NOTE TO 7

1. According to *Ching Te Chuan Teng Lu*, 9, when Liang Sui (eighth–ninth century) went to Ma Yu (Pao Ch'e, a successor of Ma Tsu), the latter called to him, "Liang Sui," whereat Liang Sui replied. Ma Yu called him thus three times and Liang Sui replied three times; finally Ma Yu said, "This stupid preacher!" Then Liang Sui was awakened. According to the later *Wu Teng Hui Yuan*, 4, when Ma Yu saw Liang Sui coming, he immediately took a hoe and went to work at hoeing up weeds. When Liang Sui came to where he was hoeing, Ma Yu paid no attention to him but immediately went back to his room and shut the door. The next day Liang Sui went to Ma Yu again, but again Ma Yu shut his door; when Liang Sui knocked, Ma Yu asked, "Who is it?" Liang Sui said, "It is Liang Sui." The moment he had called out his name, he suddenly attained enlightenment. He said to Ma Yu, "Master, do not fool Liang Sui; if I had not come to pay my respects to you, I would probably have been deceived by the sutras and shastras all my life." When he returned to his lecture hall, Liang Sui said to the congregation there, "Everything that you people know, I know; but what I know, you people do not know."

NOTES TO 8

1. This consists of recital of the Buddhist precepts, during which the monks are supposed to reveal their own transgressions.

2. The Choenji text has it, "You will regret that you didn't practice the Way when the pain was less."

NOTES TO 9

1. The Dragon Gate is actually not in the sea, but is a gorge through which the Yellow River passes at the border of Shensi and Shansi, in China. It is traditionally said to have been cut by the legendary King Yu (2206–2198 B.C.) to save China from the flooding of the Yellow River. According to legend, on the third day of the third month, when the peach blossoms are in bloom, if a fish can get past the Dragon Gate, he will become a dragon; those who cannot make it fall back and smash their heads. Hsueh Tou (980–1052) once composed this verse:

> In the river country the spring wind doesn't blow;
> Deep within the flowers partridges are calling.
> At the treble Dragon Gate when the waves are high,
>   fish become dragons;
> Yet fools still drag through the evening gutter water.

> *(Po Tse Sung Ku, 7)*

2. Or, thought after thought.

NOTE TO 10

1. Better known as Genshin (942–1003), a master of Tendai Buddhism was one of the pioneers of Pure Land Buddhism in Japan with his work *Ojoyoshu* (''Compendium of the Essentials of Salvation''), in which he traces Pure Land doctrine and practice in sutras and shastras already recognized as authoritative in Tendai Buddhism.

NOTES TO 11

1. Fujiwara Yorimichi (992–1074), regent for the emperor. A similar story is told of the fourteenth century Zen monk Ikkyu, and the Sufi figure Mulla Nasrudin.
2. From the *Hsiao Ching,* ''Classic of Filial Piety.''
3. From the *Hsiao Ching.*